# The Symbolic Tradition
# of Freemasonry

# Also from Westphalia Press

westphaliapress.org

# The Symbolic Tradition of Freemasonry

Volume 2, Number 2 of *Ritual, Secrecy, and Civil Society*

Edited by Pierre Mollier

WESTPHALIA PRESS

An imprint of Policy Studies Organization

**The Symbolic Tradition of Freemasonry: Volume 2, Number 2 of** *Ritual, Secrecy, and Civil Society*
All Rights Reserved © 2014 by Policy Studies Organization

**Westphalia Press**
An imprint of Policy Studies Organization
1527 New Hampshire Ave., NW
Washington, D.C. 20036
info@ipsonet.org

**ISBN-13: 978-1-63391-743-9**
**ISBN-10: 1633917436**

Cover design by Taillefer Long at Illuminated Stories:
www.illuminatedstories.com

Daniel Gutierrez-Sandoval, Executive Director
PSO and Westphalia Press

Cheryl Walker, Development and Programs Associate
PSO and Westphalia Press

Updated material and comments on this edition
can be found at the Westphalia Press website:
www.westphaliapress.org

*Ritual, Secrecy, and Civil Society*
Volume 2, Number 2, Winter 2014

# Table of Contents

*Note: Images referenced in this article may be viewed by scanning the code provided or visiting http://www.ipsonet.org/images/Open_Access/RSCS/RSCS_2-2_Images.pdf

# *Ritual, Secrecy and Civil Society:*
## Issue No. 4, Winter 2014

### Freemasonry, Symbolism and Society

### *Foreword* by Pierre Mollier, Editor-in-Chief

*itual, Secrecy and Civil Society* aims to provide a bridge between European and American Masonic research. This is why our review is heavily involved in the major international masonic history conference which will take place in Paris, in the prestigious setting of France's National Library, on May 29 and May 30, 2015. It will be an important event, bringing together the world's key players in Masonic studies. We hope to see you there!

The conference will focus particularly on the history of rituals, and especially on the sources of the Ancient and Accepted Scottish Rite. In preparation for this work, this issue begins with a study of a French manuscript which lies at the origin of the Francken Manuscript. Dated 1764, the "Santo-Domingo Manuscript" presents the rituals and the Masonic system spread by Stephen Morin in the Caribbean at the very beginning of the Rite of Perfection. In particular, it includes the oldest ritual, with a magnificent trestle board for the Degree of the Royal Secret, of which we publish a transcript. This is followed by an in-depth study on the sources of this astonishing trestle toard of the Royal Secret, by Dominique Jardin. This analysis clearly shows how Freemasonry re-used old material to create a new symbolic tradition.

Our review pays especial attention to the way in which Freemasonry has influenced society. The Orders and decorations of different states have a dual nature, both political and symbolic. The French example stands out for us, because the Freemasons were very active in the foundation of the Legion of Honor, the famous decoration created by Napoleon.

Finally, Freemasons have always taken an interest in the Orient. This is firstly because their rituals explain that "Light comes from the East." It is also because since the Renaissance, Westerners have been convinced that the Ancient Orient is the birthplace of the idea of initiation. Thierry Zarcone shows us the links between Freemasonry and the foundation of modern Orientalism at the end of the eighteenth century and start of the nineteenth century. He begins by presenting to us the figure of the linguist and philologist, Antoine Sylvestre de Sacy (1758–1838), a highly atypical Mason and one of the fathers of Orientalism.

# The 1764 Santo Domingo Manuscript: A Reflection of the French Original of the Francken Manuscript

Pierre Mollier[A]

The "Francken Manuscript" is the reference text for the series of high Masonic degrees that was spread by Henry Andrew Francken (c. 1720–1795) in Jamaica and then on the East Coast of the United States at the end of the eighteenth century. It is therefore an important document on the origins of the Ancient and Accepted Scottish Rite, which is currently the world's most practiced system of high degrees. Francken owed his Masonic system to Étienne (Stephen) Morin, a very active French dignitary in the Caribbean (where there were many French people in the eighteenth century). Morin had received a patent to spread these high degrees in the New World in Paris in 1761, and established them in Santo Domingo (Haiti) between his arrival on the island in January 1763 and his death in 1771. The Masons at the time knew them as the *Masonry of Perfection* or *Order of the Royal Secret*. Since the nineteenth century, historians have adopted the name *Rite of Perfection*, which can be found at the top of the Francken Manuscript.

Nobody doubted that the Francken Manuscript had French sources. In fact, it offers degrees that are shown by all the archives to have developed in France before being exported widely, and particularly into American Masonry by Morin and Francken and via the Antilles. However, the document that I wish to bring to the attention of historians here is much more than a collection of eighteenth-century French high degrees. By its very nature, it shows strong analogies with the Francken Manuscript. Whole sections of the text are identical to that of the Francken Manuscript. This even applies to the errors, such as that stating that Clement VI (not Clement V) was the pope who abolished the Order of the Temple. This document comes from Jean Baylot's collection, and is now kept in the Masonic section of France's National Library, under the reference "Baylot FM[4] 15"[1]. The specific nature and interest of this document have already been pointed out. In 1972, Paul Naudon identified it as a major source on the Rite of Perfection in the Antilles in the eighteenth century.[2] In 1997, I highlighted

[A] Director of the Grand Orient de France Library and of the Museum of Freemasonry (Paris).

[1] In issue 2891 of the *Bibliotheca Esoterica* (Dorbon), there is a Masonic manuscript with great similarities to the 1764 manuscript. A happy accident put me in touch with its current owner, who was kind enough to make it available to me. After an in-depth examination, I can state that it is undoubtedly an early nineteenth-century copy of the 1764 Santo Domingo Manuscript.

[2] Paul Naudon, "Nouvelles recherches sur les origines du Rite de Perfection," *Travaux Villard de Honnecourt* 7 (1972): 71–76; and Naudon, *Histoire, Rituels, et Tuileur des Hauts-Grades Maçonniques, Le Rite Écossais Ancien et Accepté* (Paris: Dervy-Livres, 1978), presented on page 122 and transcription of an extract on pages 423–427.

its close links to the Francken Manuscript.[3] More recently, Louis Trébuchet has assigned it an important place in the history of the Ancient and Accepted Scottish Rite.[4]

It is a nineteen-centimeter-wide by twenty-one-centimeter-high volume, bound in worn, dark-red Morocco leather. It contains seventy-four folios in laid-paper booklets, though it is difficult to tell how many booklets it contains (there may be four, five, or six of them, of different thicknesses). The watermark is only partially visible, but it seems to show a four beneath a sort of square, scalloped coat of arms featuring a hunting horn and its strap, the two sections of which cross in a gamma shape. At the end of the volume, there are three plates. An introductory note on the Knight of the Sun ritual allows the book to be dated back to 1764, and its origins to be traced to Santo Domingo.

> *The degree of Knight of the Eagle and of the Sun or the Managed Chaos, final key of the renewed Masonry. Called the 21st degree after which the only superior is the Sublime Order\* preceded by the Grand Master Elect who covers it under the title of Grand Inspector of the Lodges. This degree was given to me by the Lodge constituted for the Foix Regiment while we were camped by the great river on March 29, 1764 /and to our Lodge to the East of Saint Marc by Brother Peyrottes/ written at the camp of the great river in the headland in Santo Domingo in June 1763 [for 1764?].*

We owe the identification of Peyrottes to Alain Bernheim, who tells us what we can glean from Moreau de Saint-Méry's *Description topographique, physique, civile, politique et historique de la partie française de l'isle Saint-Domingu* (*Topographical, Physical, Civil, Political, and Historical Description of the French Part of the Island of Santo Domingo*) (Paris, 1797–1798). Peyrottes was a surveyor in Saint-Marc in 1750 (page 131) and was appointed general surveyor of the French part of Santo Domingo on March 6, 1760 (page 102), then replaced in 1768. The last page of our manuscript ends with the note "to the East of Port-au-Prince, May 9, 1768." From all of these elements, we can establish that this source came from a French Mason in Santo Domingo, a soldier who belonged to the Foix Regiment ("the Lodge constituted for the Foix Regiment while we were camped by the great river") but who later left it to remain on the island. The "Foix Infantry" was in fact sent to Santo Domingo in 1760, but returned to France in July 1765. It also appears that it was written between 1764 and 1768. A note at the top of the volume, written at the start of the nineteenth century, states that:

> *This manuscript which is missing four degrees, Apprentice, Fellow, Master, and the 1st elect or the elect of the 9, was very probably copied by an officer of the Foix regiment, from 1760 to 1770, who had to do garrison duty with his regiment in Santo Domingo. In particular, it offers the degrees of the Rite of Heredom or Perfection (in 25 degrees) as seen in the*

---

[3] Pierre Mollier, "Nouvelles Lumières sur la Patente Morin et le Rite de Perfection," *Renaissance Traditionnelle* 110–111 (1997): 125–127 (second publication in *1804–2004 Deux siècles de Rite Écossais Ancien Accepté en France* [Paris: Dervy, 2004]).

[4] Louis Trébuchet, *De l'Écosse à l'Écossisme, fondements historiques du Rite Écossais Ancien Accepté*, t.2, *Floraison des grades écossais*, 1:148–151 and transcription of numerous degrees in vol. 2, 683–931.

*Convent of Bordeaux in 1762, as well as a very small number of degrees used in the Ancient and Accepted Scottish Rite, which was copied from the above rite and organized only in 1804.*[5]

Clearly, this note was written at least forty years later than the manuscript. Nevertheless, it was written in a period that is much closer to the manuscript's era than our own, and above all at a time when in France, particularly in Paris, there were many people who had lived in Santo Domingo at the end of the eighteenth century. It is for all these reasons that I propose to refer to it hereafter as the "1764 Santo Domingo Manuscript."

It describes the rituals for the degrees of: Secret Master; Perfect Master; Secret Master by Curiosity or Intimate Secretary; Provost and Judge or Irish Master; Grand Master Architect; Scottish Trinitarian (Apprentice, Fellow, and Master); Master Elect or Little Elect; Master Elect of the Fifteen; The Elect of the Twelve—Sublime Elect—Council of the Illustrious Elect; Knight of the Royal Arch; Patriarch and Knight of the Sun Grand Master of the Light; Knight of the Lion; Knight of the Orient; Knight of the Orient and the West Prince of Jerusalem; Grand Master and Venerable of all the Lodges; Knight of the Eagle and the Pelican; Noachite Knight; second degree of Rose-Croix or Clavi Masonry; degrees of Postulant, Champion, and Great; Sublime Scottish Last Point of Perfection; Master *ad Vitam* of the Lodges of France and England; Prince of Jerusalem; Knight of the Royal Axe; Knight of the Eagle and of the Sun or the Managed Chaos; Grand Inspector of the Lodges Grand Elect Knight Kadosh; Assembly of the Sublime Princes; Discourse, Catechism of the Apprentice and Fellow Elect Cohen.

The poor quality of the manuscript, with its generally confused and rough appearance, cramped writing that is hard to read, terrible use of capitals, crossings out, overcrowding, and multiple cross-references, probably explains why this document has never been studied in detail, despite having been known to exist for forty years. It feels more like a working document, or the personal notes of a dedicated Mason, than a traditional collection of degrees. In any case, it is very different from the well-organized 1783 Francken Manuscript, with its rituals and careful calligraphy, presented in the exact order of the hierarchy of the Rite. Analyzing the 1764 Santo Domingo Manuscript presents many difficulties. Several objections can be made to contest its relationship to the Francken Manuscript. For example, interposed in the traditional scale of the Rite of Perfection are degrees not seen in the Francken Manuscript, such as the "Scottish Trinitarian," the "Patriarch of the Crusades," the "Knight of the Lion," or even, at the end of the work, rituals of the theurgical Order of the Elect Cohens. The traditional degrees of the Rite Perfection sometimes have a significantly different name, which makes their identification somewhat uncertain upon a first reading. Examples include "Master Elect, Little Elect," which is in fact a classic "Elect of the Nine;" or "Elect of the Twelve-Sublime Elect," which is the "Sublime Knight Elect" of the Francken Manuscript. Only an in-depth analysis of the texts reveals the extreme proximity of the 1764

---

[5] This comment also shows that at the start of the nineteenth century, Masonic contemporaries of the establishment of the Ancient and Accepted Scottish Rite in Paris saw the 1764 Santo Domingo manuscript as a founding document for their tradition.

Santo Domingo Manuscript to the Francken Manuscript and to it alone, out of the hundreds of Enlightenment Masonic rituals that can be consulted in the many archival collections today. It caught my attention when I studied the degree of Knight of the Sun; I noticed that in the *corpus* of around fifty eighteenth-century rituals that I had identified only this manuscript had almost the same text as the Francken Manuscript. I then made the same comparisons for the degrees of Secret Master,[6] Knight of the East,[7] and so forth. The results were identical. For the degree of Knight Kadosh,[8] the demonstration is, if possible, even more convincing. Aside from the positioning of a paragraph spanning a few lines, and two short missing sections, the texts of the rituals in the two works, even though they are around twenty pages long in cramped writing, are exactly the same! In contrast, the twenty or so eighteenth-century Kadosh rituals that I have collected are all significantly or very clearly different. Moreover, only the Knight Kadosh rituals in the 1764 Santo Domingo Manuscript and the Francken Manuscript contain certain extremely characteristic details, such as the notable error stating that Clement VI (rather than Clement V) was the Pope who abolished the Order of the Temple, or a curious list of books on the history of the Templars that the Brothers are invited to consult.

The final element supporting this close link is the presence in the 1764 Santo Domingo Manuscript not (unfortunately) of a complete ritual, but of a text relating to the degree of Prince of the Royal Secret (the first such text known). Folio 69 features a long development entitled "Ralliement des Princes Sublimes" ("Assembly of the Sublime Princes"). As the last page of the manuscript is certified to be from May 9, 1768, we can consider that the degree of the Royal Secret therefore dates back to the period before 1768. The small note at the top of the ritual of the Knight of the Sun takes us back four more years. The Knight of the Sun is described as the "21st degree after which the only superior is the Sublime Order* preceded by the Grand Master Elect who covers it under the title of Grand Inspector of the Lodges." This convoluted wording first gives us the following succession to the top of the system: Knight of the Sun, Grand [Master] Elect Grand Inspector (the traditional name for the Kadosh), and the "Sublime Order*" that the author does not dare name, but which must refer to the "Assembly of the Sublime Princes" described just after the Kadosh ritual in our manuscript.

Yet this comment was "written at the camp of the great river in June 1763 [for 1764]." This shows that the "Royal Secret" existed and was practiced in Santo Domingo in 1764, when Etienne Morin, who a few months before had returned from a long journey, spread his system on the island. In fact, it is my belief that the whole series of "Scottish" degrees (that is, almost the whole manuscript, which displays a certain unity) was copied in 1764. Only the last few pages on the Elect Cohen were added later, in 1768. This document therefore gives a fixed

---

[6] Pierre Mollier and Jacques Léchelle, "Le Manuscrit Saint-Domingue 1764 à la source du manuscrit Francken—I. Le grade de Maître Secret," *Renaissance Traditionnelle* 113 (1998): 31–45.

[7] Pierre Mollier and Jacques Léchelle, "Le Manuscrit Saint-Domingue 1764 à la source du manuscrit Francken—II. Le grade de Chevalier d'Orient," *Renaissance Traditionnelle* 114 (1998): 123–151.

[8] Pierre Mollier and Jacques Léchelle, "Le Manuscrit Saint-Domingue 1764 à la source du manuscrit Francken—III. Le grade de Grand Inspecteur Grand Élu ou Chevalier Kadosh," *Renaissance Traditionnelle* 120 (1999): 234–277.

testimony of the practice of the Rite of Perfection at the time when Etienne Morin implanted it between Santo Domingo and Jamaica. Undoubtedly, it even came from a Brother in his entourage: the presence of the "Royal Secret" (which the copyist did not initially dare to name explicitly) shows that he was allowed into the very heart of Morin's system.

Therefore, the text on the Royal Secret—this "Assembly of the Sublime Princes," which, although not a complete ritual as such, contains all the elements of one—very probably comes from Étienne Morin himself. The magnificent illustration of the "camp of the Princes," which is one of the three plates included in the manuscript, also dates back to 1764. Initially, since it is a very careful piece of work that contrasts with the rough style of the 1764 Santo Domingo Manuscript, I thought that it had been added later on, perhaps even by its owner in the early nineteenth century (the author of the note making the link with the Ancient and Accepted Scottish Rite). However, an in-depth examination of the way the plates have been stuck in at the end of the volume reveals that everything goes together, and that this plate was not a later addition. Importantly (and movingly), its forty-one-centimeter by forty-five-centimeter dimensions and the strong paper chosen suggest that it is probably a real painting that was used in ceremonies.

Is the 1764 Santo Domingo Manuscript the French original from which the Francken Manuscript was copied? No, because if it was, how would we explain the missing sections and the few (admittedly minor, but real) differences between the two documents? It seems more like a testimony on the Rite of Perfection in 1764, and therefore naturally has close links to the French original of the Francken Manuscript. It is even possible to envisage the following hypothesis: the 1764 Santo Domingo Manuscript reflects the state of the Rite of Perfection in 1764, when there were only 23 degrees, as specified in the note at the top of the Knight of the Sun ritual. This early state might actually help to explain its "rough" aspect. Étienne Morin honed and added to his system between 1764 and 1765–68, when it had 25 degrees, and conferred it to Henry Andrew Francken.

The 1764 Santo Domingo Manuscript therefore appears as a very important document on the beginnings of the Rite of Perfection, and therefore as an essential source on the origins of the Ancient and Accepted Scottish Rite.

# The Nec plus ultra Or 25th degree called The Royal Secret or the knights of St. Andrews, and the Faithful guardians of the Sacred Treasurer

## Francken Ms, 1783 copy

Preparations and decorations for fitting out the apartment necessary for holding of a gr$^d$ chapter, or council of the sovereign prince of the Royal Secret.

This gr$^d$ chapt$^r$ must be held somewhere in an open country on a rising ground, and in a building of at least two stories high. On the 2$^d$ floor of which must be 3 apartments, where in the grand chapter is to be held, & such a meeting in day time, & not at night.

1$^{st}$ the 2 Tilers, are to be on the first floor or ground, one to tile Every where, and the other on the stairs. The first chamber up stairs is for the guards; the 2$^d$ apartment for preparing the cand$^{te}$ and the 3$^d$ is that for the chapter, or reception.

This apartment is to be hung with black Sattin bestrewed with silver Tears. Skeletons, Thigh bones across and dead heads.

2$^{dly}$ There must be a Throne Erected, in the East, under which is a chair of State, for the Sovereign of Sovereigns & gr$^d$ Ill. Prince who is the commander in chief – This Throne is to be ascended by 5 steps, and lined also with black satin, with firy flames instead of Tears; and before the sovereign is a table, cover'd with black satin with Tears; and on the forepart of the cloth a dead head on 2 bones across with the initials IM, the I over the head, and the M under the Bones –

3$^{dly}$ The Sovereign gr$^d$ Commander is to be armed with a bucler and a naked sword, the sceptre and a balance on the table before him, without any books excepted our laws.

4$^{thly}$ In the west facing the gr$^d$ Commander are placed the 2 gr$^d$ wardens by the title of Lieut-$^{nt}$ commd$^{rs}$. They are to wear buclers, and their hats on as well as the gr$^d$ commd$^r$, their sword across on a table before them; and this table cover'd with a crimson satin border'd with black ditto, bestrew'd with silver Tears; and on the forepart of said table, these initials NKMK, embroidered in golden Letters –

5$^{thly}$ The Minister of State stands on the right hand of the Sovereign, and acts as gr$^d$ orator –

6$^{thly}$ The gr$^d$ chancellor, on the left of the sovereign

7$^{thly}$ Next the minister of state stands the Gr$^d$ Secretary

8$^{thly}$ Next the chancellor, stands the gr$^d$ Treasurer

9$^{thly}$ below them on one side is placed the Ensigneur [for "Enseigneur", standard bearer?] who at the same time is the gr$^d$ M$^r$ architect – and opposite him on the other side, the captain of the guards -&

10$^{thly}$ Six member stands below these, dressed in red, without aprons; but all of them wearing the jewel of the order on theit breast, suspended to a large broad black ribbon in a triangular form.

# Manuscrit Saint-Domingue 1764 (BnF, Fd maçonnique, Baylot FM⁴ 15)

[The beginning of the Francken mauscript has no equivalent in the 1764 Santo-Domingo manuscript.]

*The Royal Secret, or the Rendevous of the Sublime Prince ---*

Instructions for the Re-union of the Brothers knights, Princes and Commanders of the Royal Secret or Kadoch, which signifies the Holy Brothers separated.

Frederic the 3rd king of Prussia, grand Master and commander in chief sovereign of sovereign &c &c with an army composed of the knights Prince of the white and black Eagle, Including Prussians, English and French likewise joined by the Prince of Libanus or the Royal Ax, the knights of Rose cross or St Andrew, Knts of East & West, the Princes of Jerusalem, knts of East, the grd Elected perfect & sublime, knts of the Royal arch, knts sublme Elected &c &c &c.

The description of the draught or camp –

The equilateral triangle in the center of the draft represents the centre of the army and shews where the knights of Malta are to be placed / who have been admitted into our mysteries / who have shewn themselves faithful guardians of the order – They are to be joyned with the knights of the white and black Eagle.

The corps in the pentagone, is to be commanded by 5 princes who are to take the command, joyntly, or by rotations according to their degrees, and receives their orders immediately from the sovereign of sovereigns grd Mer Commander in chief.

These 5 Princes shall fix their standers in the 5 angles of the pentagon, represented in the above drought in the following manner (vist.)

1st the standard or flag T, bearing arms as golden Lion, holding in his mouth a golden key, and wearing a golden collar with these letters on said collar S.Q.S. – Said Lion in an azure field; at the bottom of said flag these word ad majorem Dei gloriam.

2d The Standard or flag E. bearing arms an Inflamed heart with gules, sable winged, crowned with a laurel Syn cope [pour sinople ?] -- the field argent.

3d The Standard or flag N. bearing arms a spread Eagle – with two heads, a glden crown connecting both heads – in a form of a collar. Said Eagle holding a naked sword – in his right claw the point downwards and a bloody heart in his left claw – the field light green.

4th The Standard or flag G. Bearing an Ox sable, in a field of or /or gold/.

5th The flag or Standard U. bearing the Ark of the covenant, with 2 light green palmtrees, in a Purple Field; at the bottom of the flag, these words Laus Deo –

The Heptagon represented above, points out the Encampment of the Princes of Libannus & Jerusalem who are to receive their order from the princes abovemention'd

The Eneagon represented above, is the encampment of the masons of all denominations as shall be explained hereafter – Note: That every tent represents a whole camp; and the flags & Pendants points out the different degrees of Masonry; and each letter distinguishes the flags is taken from these words which we made use of in this sublime degree – thus the degree of the Rose=Cross or St Andrews, or white Eagle will be distinguished by a white flag and pendant Stained a little with red – and is represented by the FLAG S.

*Ralliement des princes sublimes*

Frédéric III roy de Prusse grand maître et commandant général avec son armée. Les princes sublimes français anglais et prussiens. Les chevaliers de St André d'Ecosse et les gardiens fidèles du temple.

Le triangle [triangle avec un point au centre] représente le centre ou seront les chevaliers de malthe qui se joindront à nous et se faisant connaître les gardiens fidèles de notre thrésor secret. à leur tête sera le prince, ou à son default, les princes ... tous les cinq successivement l'un à l'autre et par rang d'ancienneté ou tous les cinq ensemble et recevront l'ordre directement du roy de prusse.

Ils occuperont le [pentagone avec un 5 au centre] à chaque angle duquel sont les cinq pavillons scavoir ou le
T au lion d'or tenant à la gueule une clef d'or et ayant un collier d'or avec les lettres S.Q.S. sur un fond d'azur et au bas les lettres initiales de ces mots Ad Majorem Dei Gloria.
E au cœur enflammé de gueule ailé de sable et couronné de lauriers sinople fond d'argent.
N à l'aigle à deux têtes une couronne d'or servant de collier au deux cols ensemble tenant une épée de la serre droite la pointe en bas sur un fond sinople
G au bœuf de sable fond d'or.
U à l'arche d'Alliance d'or deux palmiers sinoples le fond pourpre avec ces mots Laus Deo
Le [heptagone avec un 7 au centre] est pour les princes du Liban et les princes de Jérusalem ceux cy recevront les ordres des premiers qui les recevront des princes sublimes.
#Chaque lettre pour indiquer chaque grade par tente ainsi que chaque lettre pour indiquer les étendards ou pav[ois]
Le [ennéagone avec un 9 au centre] est pour les neufs camps des maçons en tous grades suivant l'arrangement cy après
NB que chaque tente représente un camp et les pavois et pavillons la couleur du grade. Chaque pavillons cy dessus sont prises des trois mots consacrés aux seules cérémonies sublimes

1st Tent S. Called Malachias, and shews the camp of the knight of East and West, & Princes of Jerusalem

2d Tent A Called Zurrubabel has a light green flag & Pendant and shews the camp of the knts of the East or Sword

3d L Called Nehemias, has a red flag and Pendant, and represents the camp of the grd Eld Perf & Sublime

4th Tent I, Called Homen, has a black & red flag & Pendant, and represents the camp of the knts of the Royal Arch

5th Tent X. Called Phaleg, has a black flag & Pendant and represents the camp of the Elected of 9, of 15 and the illusd knights

6th Tent N. Called Joyadas, has a red and black flag and pendant represents the camp of the Prevosts & Judges –

7th O. Called Eliab, has a green & red flag & Pendant and points out the camp of the Intends of the buildings & Intimate Secretary –

8th N, Called Jusue, has a green flag & pendant, & shews the camp of the Perfect & Secret masters –

9th Tent S I Called Esdras, has a blue flag & Pendant and Shews the camp of the Symbolic masons and the volunteers.

The hour fixed on, shall be the 5th after the sun set and shall be known by the firing of 5 great guns, one first by itself, and 4 more at equal distance and bristly.

The 1st Rendevous shall be at the port of Naples, from then for the 2d to the port of Rhodes, and from Rhodes to Cyprus & Malta where the whole Naval Force of all nations is to assemble – the 3d at Joppa and the land forces rendevous is to be at Jerusalem, when they will be to joyned by our faithful guardians there.

The names of our Standard bearer are Bezeleel, Eliab, Menchem, Garinous & Emerk

The watch words for every day in the week are as folld and there are not to be changed but to the express order from the king of Prussia.

| | Challenging | Protectors of Masons Each day and word | Prophets |
|---|---|---|---|
| Sunday | | Cyrus | Ezechiel |
| Monday | | Darius | Daniel |
| Tuesday | | Xerxes | Habacuck |
| Wednesday | | Alexander | Sophonias |
| Thursday | | Philadelphus | Aggeus |
| Friday | | Herod | Zacharias |
| Saturday | | Ezechias | Malachi |

Passwords

D. Polcat, Wch signifies/ which means, separated

A. Pharaskal wch means, Reunited & accomplish –

Then they both say: Nika, Mika, signifying, I will be the revenger

S. au pavillon et pavois blanc flamme rouge représente le camp des chevaliers rose-croix ou de l'aigle blanc ou St André d'Ecosse

A. au pavillon et pavois vert d'eau représente le camp des chevaliers d'orient.

L au pavillon et pavois rouge représente le camp des grands élus parfait maître et sublime écossois

I au pavillon et pavois noir et rouge représente le camp des Elus, maître Elu et chevaliers Elus chevaliers de la Royale Arche.

X. au pavillon et pavois noir représente le camp des Elus, maîtres Elus et chevaliers Elus.

N. au pavillon et pavois bandes rouges et noires représente le camp des maîtres irlandois.

O au pavillon et pavois bandes vertes et rouges représente le camp des maîtres anglais.

N. au pavillon et pavois vert représente le camp des maîtres parfaits.

S. au pavillon et pavois bleu représente le camp des maîtres symboliques et volontaires


Les noms des neufs camps sont.

S. malachias. A. Zorobabel. L nehemias. I. homen X. phaleg. N. joyada. O. Eliab. N. josué. S. Esdras.


## Heures indiquées

La cinquième après soleil couché par cinq coups de canon ainsi tirés 1 et 4.


## Rendés-vous

A paris au temple, à naples au palais royal, à rome au capitole, à malthe à l'hotel. en mer à l'isle de chypre ou se rendra l'armée navale de toutes les nations. Après avoir passé pour second rendez-vous au port de malthe, et le troisième rendez-vous est à jerusalem ou sont nos gardiens fidèles.


Les noms des gardes –Etendards sont beseleel, Eliab, Menahem, garimont et Emerk.

Les mots de l'orde pour chaque jour de la semaine qui ne changeront que par la volonté du roy de prusse commandant général sont ainsi


| Demandes prophètes | | Les protecteurs sont | |
| --- | --- | --- | --- |
| Dimanche | Ezechiel | | Cyrus |
| Lundi | daniel | | darius |
| Mardy | Habacuc | | Xercéz |
| Mercredi | Sophonie | | alexandre |
| Jeudy | aggée | | philadelphe |
| Vendredy | Zacharie | | herode |
| Samedy | malachie | | Ezechias |

Les mots de passe sont

Demande      poolkal….Séparés

Réponse      pharaskal..réunis

Ils disent ensemble NIKA MEKA

Explanation of the Tents and their Letters

The Tent S. of the kn<sup>ts</sup> of East & west &c at the top of the draught, go from that round against the sun and read on when you will find the words Salix Nonis.

The camp of the Pentagon, read as above, and you will find the word Tengu.

These three words Joyned, form the Initials of the following Prophecy in French /viz<sup>t</sup>/ Soutenons aprésent L'Invincible Xerxes, Nous offer Notre Incomparable Sacré Trésor, Et nous gagnerons Victorieusement

Which is attempted in English by H. A. Francken thus Support adversity Le Invincible Xerxes Now offered Near Incomparable Sacred Treasure Engaged, Now gives Victory.

To open and close the gr<sup>d</sup> chapter or Consistory The President says Salix, The 2 grd officers say Nonis, then all together say Tengu which signifies the Rallying of the wise brethren, who have been hitherto separated.

The sign is you put your right hand on your heart, then hold it up, and then let it fall on your right side, which sign is made by them altogether

The Sublime Prince will have the possession of our Treasure, as being the old Treasure of the order; and the knights of Malta who will joyn us, shall have and Enjoy the same honors & Privileges –

The Prince of Jerusalem, shall be honored with the degree of white & black Eagle, and will command the knights of the East, the scotch, the symbolic's and the volunteers, with the password Tripple Pronounced and Elchadai, w<sup>ch</sup> word signifies Delta

Let us imitate our grand Master Hiram Abif who, to the last placed all his hope in the great architect of the universe, and pronounced the following words, just as he past from this transient life into Eternal Bliss

Spes mea In deo Est

Finis

[Sceau]

H. A. Franchen Pr. Of the R: St. and Senior Depty grd Inspr over all Lodges, Council, Chapters & over the two Hemispheres –

In Kingston Jamaica, in the year of light near the B:B. 7783

Les mots pour ouvrir et fermer le Conseil Souverain des princes sublimes sont. Le premier officier dit SALIX le second dit NONIS et le troisième TENGU qui signifie ralliement des ffr. Sages

Toutes les lettres de ces mots de l'ouverture  du conseil prises l'une après l'autre sont les initiales de cette prophétie. <u>S</u>outenons <u>à</u>présent ; l'<u>in</u>vincible  <u>X</u>ercès <u>nous</u> <u>offre</u> <u>notre</u> in<u>comparable</u> <u>thrésor</u> <u>sacré</u> <u>et</u> <u>nous</u> <u>g</u>agnerons <u>v</u>ictorieusement……. Les princes sublimes posséderont les thrésor comme anciens temp. Et les chevaliers de malthe qui l'y joindront auront les mêmes honneurs et prérogatives

Les princes de Jérusalem seront reçus commandeurs de l'aigle noir et commanderont les chevaliers de l'orient, les grand Ecossois les symboliques et les volontaires avec le mot de passe à triple prononciation
Imitons notre grand maître qui jusqu'à la fin mit son espérance au grand architecte de l'univers et proféra ces dernières paroles en passant d'ici à la gloire <u>Spes</u> <u>mea</u> <u>in</u> <u>deo</u> <u>est</u>
La partie supérieure du frontispice est <u>virtute</u> <u>et</u> <u>Silentio</u>
Le signe se fait en levant les bras ouvert les mains renversées les doigts écartés et les laisser retomber sur les cuisses. L'aigle qui ouvre ses ailes en signe de protection pour les ordres qui lui sont soumis.

Fin

# The Iconography of the Lodge Tracing Board of the Thirty-Second Degree of the AASR, Sublime Prince of the Royal Secret

Dominique Jardin[A]

Note: To view images referenced in this article, scan the code above or visit: http://www.ipsonet.org/images/Open_Access/RSCS/RSCS_2-2_Images.pdf

The seal and/or tracing board of the degree of Sublime Prince of the Royal Secret have not, it would seem, yet been the object of a specific or heraldic study. A specific lodge tracing board of the degree has not been identified, though it is stated in one of the first rituals[1] that it should be drawn on the floor in the middle of the lodge:

> In the middle of the apartment a Nonagon shall be traced whose every corner will be indicated by one of the letters SALIX NONI. . . . In the Nonagon a heptagon will be drawn and in it a pentagon. . . . In the Pentagon a triangle will be placed, and in it a circle that will designate the space occupied by the Princes of the Royal Secret.

There are iconographic representations of these designs and patterns on paper. They are referred to as a "camp" or "seal," and, by extension, "lodge tracing board." The latter case is not a lodge carpet laid on the ground, but rather a tracing board presented to the East, in front of the Grand Commander's desk. There are also some rare old aprons that bear the camp's motif. This motif, the composition of which is

---

[A] University of Mannheim

[1] The ritual that I use here is, unless otherwise stated, the manuscript of the Bibliothèque nationale de France listed under *Nouv. Acq. Frçs* 10960 (the Cabinet des Manuscrits series entitled Nouvelles Acquisitions Françaises, and therefore not part of the Masonic collection). The title of the ritual, which can be dated to between 1810 and 1825, is *Knight of Saint Andrew, Faithful Keeper of the Sacred Treasure and Valiant Prince of the Royal Secret*. It has sometimes been called "Morin," a name that has in fact nothing to do with Morin and that I will not use here.

beautiful, with its colors and the movement from the wind that makes its flags flutter, is enigmatic, complex, and fundamental for understanding the degree. The ritual gives us a detailed but "literal" and descriptive explanation of it that does not seem to cover all of its meanings.

The story of the degree depicts a powerful army, consisting of corps sheltered in tents that are "placed in a nonagon" on the one hand, and a pentagon on the other, so as to build a camp. The recipient is questioned by each of the heads of the various army corps, who correspond to different high degrees and are sheltered under tents with pennons and flags. He is then admitted to participate in the expedition to reach Jerusalem. The different army corps can then set off and form a procession, "each under the banner of its leader," before "coming to a stop" to pray before each of the five ports that punctuate the route of the expedition and that are the cause for a number of symbolic journeys. Once these journeys are over and the army has regrouped, the applicant is received as "Valiant Prince of the Royal Secret" and "Faithful Guardian of the Treasure of the Order," and he "enters the Consistory."

Things become more enigmatic when one realizes that the words of the degree are made out of the series of letters associated with each of the tents of the camp and their flags: SALIX NONIS for the outer circle and TENGU for the inner one.[2] Moreover, each of the army leaders is also the "standard bearer" and has the name of a character from the Old Testament. And the acclamation *Laus Deo* is written on what is almost certainly the most important flag of the camp, since it bears the Ark of the Covenant. The summary of degrees offered by the ritual introduces some that are not part of the AASR or the Rite of Perfection, such as Grand Pontiff, Grand Master of the Key, and Grand Patriarch. Certain iconographic representations correspond to the names of the army leaders. For example, the Ark of the Covenant flag is associated with Bezalel, which is quite consistent. But other iconographic elements are in discordance with the listed titles.

My goal here is in short both to provide a reading of the images of the flags by verifying the heraldic code—a rarity in Masonry—that they display and to propose an interpretative framework for some of the motifs. The difficulty of giving meaning to symbols must not prevent interpretative readings from being provided, provided that they are based on documents that support the reasoning given.[3] I have chosen to focus in particular on certain very discreet motifs at the center of the tracing board, and then on the standards of the inner circle of tents (TENGU), and finally on the motif of glory,

---

[2] I will not study these words in this research.

[3] The article by Ion Lazar, "The Symbolic Camp of the 32: Mysteries of Sacred Geometry & Masonic Astronomy," *Hérédom* 18 (2010): 259–297, takes as its basis of study the iconography and in particular the geometric shapes of the camp—which illustrate the cover of *Hérédom*—but it is limited to the Pike tracing board. This article does not seem to fit in with the critical historical method, but rather it favors a personal hermeneutic approach that "applies" Kabbalistic and astrological considerations and even "sacred geometry," the latter being based on Pythagorean approaches. All these considerations are external and subsequent to the oldest rituals and the oldest iconographies, which they do not take into account. Even the Cross of Saint Andrew, which is raised on pages 261 and 265, is completely absent from the first tracing boards.

which characterizes both the iconography and the ritual of the degree. For example, here I suggest reading the motif of the camp that connects the first five flags as a shrine, in the medieval sense of the word, as in a chest, in the center of the center—the tabernacle of the temple.

This reading, which highlights the tetramorph motif, does not appear to have been put forward thus far. The tetramorph is a highly original figure that is commonly known as "the Four Living Creatures"[4]—the lion, the eagle, the ox, and the human/angel. These Four Living Creatures appear in the visions of Ezekiel and John, and they are linked to Christian tradition's Four Evangelists. However, we know less about their presence, real though it is, in the Masonic realm. Here they do not surround—as should be the case—the Ark of the Covenant, which is associated with them. Instead, these Four Living Creatures enshrine both the Ark and its contents—that is, the very particular space of the center of the tracing board. That is why it is a twofold shrine; it features a twofold esoteric background that it nevertheless displays. The goal of the initiatory journey of the tracing board can be identified as Jerusalem, but it is also important to deconstruct complex and nested symbolic motifs that correspond to a very rich layering of meanings.

A general understanding of the degree must incorporate the religious context of its development at the end of the eighteenth century, as this provides a key to its construction. Although some items have disappeared from the written rituals, they remain present in the form of iconographic motifs, which are at times very discreet. I have chosen here to focus on these motifs and to propose an interpretation of them. The iconography of the lodge tracing boards underscores and selects the essential moments of the rituals and invites alternative readings of them.[5]

## I - The Iconographic Sources Used and the Structure Common to the Tracing Boards

*A. The Iconographic Sources*

My argument is based on a corpus that is limited to the "first tracing boards" (those from before the mid-nineteenth century, since later tracing boards are repetitions) found both on paper (tracing boards or seals) and on aprons. It would be appropriate to quickly introduce these according to their age. One quickly realizes that the motifs and the structure are very similar from one tracing board to another, though with some specificities that are worth noting. This is why, rather than adding to the iconographic instances of the camp, which are virtually identical or "fanciful" at the end of the nineteenth century, I would prefer to make comparisons with other lodge tracing boards or other types of sources that seem enlightening.

1) The oldest representations are in black and white. They appear in the following manuscripts:

---

[4] The Four Living Creatures can be written with or without capitals depending on the context, though generally the first letters of "Living Creatures" are capitalized.

[5] Referring back to descriptions of the armies of the camp, the passwords, their commentaries, and so forth that have been provided several times in the past is beyond the scope of this article.

a) *Ms Baylot* BNF FM4. 15, (also called *Ms St Domingue*), dated to 1764 (fig.1).

This manuscript is characterized by the imprecision of certain black-and-white representations, by its size (the camp is 25cm x 25cm, making it a true lodge tracing board), by the originality of its central motifs, and, perhaps above all, by the systematic presence of rays that transform every geometric figure into an essential motif, that of a glory.

b) *Ms Francken* (black and white, *circa* 1784, fig. 2).

This tracing board is characterized by the presence of doubled letters of the passwords on the internal face of the nonagon. These are linked to the pennons and flags that are above the tents at identical heights. The only readable motif is that of the inscription *Laus Deo.*

The Francken and Baylot manuscripts both show posts placed on the sides of the pentagon that disappear on the other tracing boards.

c) The "Thory" tracing board, *circa* 1804 (fig. 3), Latomia.

d) Vuillaume's *Tuileur* (black and white, fig. 4, 1820). This tracing board probably draws on an earlier iconography; it alternates letters and numbers on the tents and the pennons. The posts have disappeared. On the other hand, appearing under legend numbers, the dove, raven, and phoenix appear.

At their center, all these tracing boards also have very important small motifs that are subsequently seldom seen again.

2) Nineteenth-century tracing boards and aprons, in color.

a) *La Parfaite Union* Douai, early nine-teenth century; splendid color iconography (fig. 5).

This tracing board is highly original because the external pennons move from left to right, establishing a series that would be continued with the tracing boards by Pike and the Suprème Conseil de France in 1986 (not shown here), and because the flags of the inner circle flutter from right to left, which means that the winds change direction from one circle to another! This tracing board is that of the banner shown in full in fig. 10.

b) Tracing board from the Meyer Collection, in color, Library of the Grand Orient de France (fig. 6).

This tracing board, which is presented as the seal of the degree, includes the outer heraldic colors in the central circle, and once more the pennons move from right to left. However, it is not possible to determine in which direction the wind blows against the inner flags, since the stylized representation of them does not include poles.

c) Apron from the Samory collection, color, Library of the Grand Orient de France (fig. 7). This beautiful apron faithfully incorporates the heraldic colors of the tracing boards, and the flags and pennons once again move from right to left. It is worth noting the presence of the gold thread, which represents glory, on the bib and apron itself.

d) Apron from the Libert collection, color, nineteenth century (fig. 8), the defining feature of which is the inclusion of the word SALIX NONI against the wind.

e) Apron from the collection of the Museum-Library of the Grande Loge de France (fig. 9), first half of the nine-teenth century.

3) Banner held by the Museum of Freemasonry, Paris; it shows the camp and its latitudinal coordinates (no longitude is given), which correspond to the city of Douai (fig. 10).

4) Sources relating to rituals—and their iconography—other than those of the Prince of the Royal Secret must be drawn on, which show the exact origins of the flags in their Masonic form. I present these in the article or in the captions that accompany the figures.

### B. What is the Structure of the Lodge Tracing Board and How are Its Motifs Arranged?

The tracing board brings together geometric figures—circle, triangle, pentagon, heptagon, and nonagon—and motifs that for the most part are made up of flags, pennons, or gonfalons.[6] These are distributed according to the geometric figures; each bears heraldic colors and/or a motif.

The center of the composition is taken up with different motifs that vary according to the tracing boards. Most often they are very small motifs that border a strange cross with four or five branches. Flags and gonfalons are animated due to the wind making them flap, sometimes in the same direction (fig. 1, 2, 3, 4), sometimes in a different direction (fig. 5), sometimes in an indeterminate direction when they either do not have poles or they are not animated by the wind (fig. 6). The word "animated" is a very important one here, because it communicates the idea of an *anima*, a soul to these flags and a dynamic that brings them to life and places them into the three circles formed by the outer edges of the flags. The central circle is explicitly traced (fig. 1, 2, 3, 5, 6). The other two circles that are determined by lines of the outer edges of the flags (second circle) and the pennons or gonfalons (third circle) are more implicit.

The central circle is inside a pentagon that bears the five flags, which is itself inside the heptagon (which bears no flag!). The heptagon is in turn inside the nonagon, which bears the tents of the camp.

### C. The Rules of Heraldry

Pastoureau reminds us of the rules of heraldry, which are very precise and were set in the twelfth century.[7] Tinctures are divided into two groups: metals (gold, silver) on the one hand and the colors (gules = red, sable = black, azure = blue, vert = green, purpure = purple) on the other hand. It is prohibited to use two tinctures that belong to the same group together. If two tinctures overlap one must be a metal, the other a color. Exceptions to this are rare. Most often—and this is the case here—the main cross and smaller crosses are red on white background. Metals can in fact be represented by colors: gold by yellow, and silver by white. Between the beginning of the seventeenth century and the beginning of the eighteenth, a hatching system was developed that represented tinctures using

---

[6] A gonfalon—the word is used in rituals—is a battle standard and war banner, made up of a strip that comes to several points. A pennant is a small flag. A flag is a piece of cloth attached to a pole. It bears the colors of a nation or a leader to serve as a rallying point and a symbol. The word "ensign" is used in a maritime context.

[7] Pastoureau, *Traité d'héraldique*, 100–112.

strokes and dots.[8] The tracing board in Vuillaume's *Tuileur*, fig. 4, or later on the tracing boards that are not shown here, such as those of Pike, Tessier, or the Suprême Conseil de France (in 1995), use this system of hatching and dots.

## D. Movement and Dynamics of the Tracing Board

The dynamics of the top and the bottom of the scale of degrees, and of the degree of apprentice to the thirty-second degree and vice versa (since all thirty-seconds remain an apprentice and are in fact the same brothers who work in the consistory and in the blue lodge), intersects with the center-periphery dynamic according to the logic of evolution-involution. The latter also embodies a logic of distribution of power according to the *inner circle*: among the Masters, there are Scots, among the Scots, there are the Emperors of the East, and so forth. This logic, which goes from the periphery to the center, where power is specifically focused, is explicitly revealed at the thirty-second degree. From this perspective, the *rota*, the movement, which is identical to that of the dual circulation on the mysterious scale, counts as much as the journey of steps or "stations" on each of its rungs. In the particular case of the camps represented by colors, this circular—or rather, spiral—movement acquires a speed that may dissolve the colors into the white in order to achieve the "white work." This spiral and this turning movement correspond to the one that drives the wheels of the Ezekiel's chariot as they accompany each of the Four Living Creatures,

as I will examine a little later. The wheels of Ezekiel's vision (fig. 14) merge here with the great wheel of the camp, which represents the *galapal* (or whirl) brought to life by the wind that blows through the banners. This movement accompanies another that is driven by the angels, which are engaged in working the cranks that make the world go round, put *ordo* into *chaos*, and thus stabilize the cosmos (fig. 15). The banners of the camp's tents, floating in the wind according to the rotation displayed, can be considered on the poetic level of the angels' spread wings that surround Romanesque representations of the tetramorph.

The tetramorph is in fact frequently accompanied by the choir of angels or celestial armies, and the Masonic armies of the different degrees are perhaps a late and substitute iteration of these celestial armies, as they may also be of the twelve tribes of Israel, something that I will examine later in this article. This movement is essential since it determines the order defined by the degree ritual of the procession of the army corps that sets off to Jerusalem, and also because it indicates the reading order of the enigmatic forms of TENGU for the inner circle and of SALIX NONI (S) for the outer circle—unless the opposite is the case, with the order of the letters suggesting the order of the parade, independently of the direction of the wind. Accordingly, the apron of the Libert collection (nineteenth century, fig. 8) shows flags that are all fluttering due to a wind blowing from left to right, but the SALIX NONIS formula is expressed against the wind—the only example of this noted—while TENGU follows the wind.

---

[8] Gold is represented by a clustering of small dots, silver by a blank space, gules by vertical lines, azure by horizontal ones, sable by horizontal and vertical lines that intersect at right angles, vert by diagonal lines descending from left to right, and purpure by diagonal lines descending from right to left.

## II - The Center Motifs of the Lodge Tracing Board

It would be worth looking at the different symbolic motifs by beginning from the center of the tracing board in order to gradually expand the analysis to the motifs of the successive peripheries.

### A. The Triangle and the Birds

The degree's explanation of the camp says:

> The triangle that you see in the middle of the tracing board represents the center of the army, and it is the place that must be occupied by the Knights of Malta[9] who are admitted into our mysteries and who join the Knights Kadosh to share with them in watching over the treasure under the orders of the mighty Princes of the Royal Secret.

At the "center of the center" there is therefore a treasure that can only be symbolic and that perhaps—almost certainly, even—constitutes the Royal Secret.

The animals represented in the center of the composition and at the tips of the triangle are the raven, the dove, and the phoenix—representations of the stages of the Magnum Opus: black with the raven; red with the phoenix; white with the dove. The ritual explains:

> R A day will come when I will be permitted to learn more
> D On what do you base this new hope?
> R On an apparition
> D What objects were presented to you
> R 3 birds, a raven, a dove, and a phoenix
> D What does the raven announce?
> R The blackness of its plumage symbolizes anguish, disorder, and death
> D What does the dove tell you?
> R Its whiteness announces the regeneration of the creatures to me
> D What does the phoenix recall to you?
> R This bird that emerges from the flames to start a new life is the emblem of perfected nature, of a universal theory, and of boundless power.

If the dove and the raven are present from the founding episode of Noah, the phoenix and dove actively contribute here to the respiritualizing program of Creation suggested by Revelation, a book whose presence in the tracing board is hidden but real, if only by the mention of the tetramorph's animals and the figure of the heptagon.

The triangle primarily shows the importance of the Trinity; the candidate is received as Valiant Prince of the Royal Secret "in the name of the holy and indivisible Trinity."

> Then placing his sword on the head of the candidate, he says:
> In the name of the holy and indivisible Trinity, under the auspices of the Most Serene Grand Commander of the order and with the consent of the valiant princes here, I receive

---

[9] It is beyond the scope of this study to examine the relationship between the Knights of Malta and Masonic Knights.

you and make you now and for always Valiant Prince of Royal Secret, Knight of Saint Andrew, and Faithful Guardian of the Sacred Treasure.

In this regard, it is important to recall the covert but real salience of the Trinitarian mark and logic that shape the degree. Here the center becomes spiritual, since to the ritual's question: "Where are you going?" the recipient responds, "To the Orient." And he completes his response through the method used for the purpose: "Where by means of a mysterious scale, I hope to arrive at the point of glory and splendor."

The point of glory is identified with the Orient and the triangle radiating glory. Not only is the reference to glory present, as seen here, in the text of the ritual, but it also powerfully shapes the iconography.

## B. The Cross or the Five-Pointed Star

There are numerous significant and meaningful dualities in the center of the tracing board of the thirty-second degree. There is the cross that symbolizes Christ: in Romanesque art, Christ in his mandorla, or the cross, are systematically placed at the center of the tetramorph (fig 16), and on the lodge tracing board of the Strict Templar Observance (fig. 17), Hiram is at the center of the four animals! There is also a strange, five-pointed cross, which one cannot help but compare to the five-pointed star that also sometimes symbolizes Christ. The center of the circle is occupied by either a red cross (tracing board of La Parfaite Union de Douai, fig. 12B) or a "cross" with five points, which is therefore not a cross at all, but rather a star (Samory apron or *Ms Baylot*, fig. 12A). The red cross, a key Masonic motif for high degrees, is set as an X on certain tracing boards for the thirty-second degree, and thus becomes a cross of

saint Andrew, the apostle who shifted from the old law to the new.

## C. The Discreet and Essential Motifs, Placed between the Branches of the Cross or the Star

The five-pointed star or "cross" is bordered by several motifs that have not been studied or even identified so far. As far as I am aware, they are present only in the manuscripts *Baylot (FM4-15 fol. 76.)*, *Francken*, and Vuillaume's *Tuileur*. In *Ms Baylot* we can see on the one hand a compass open "downward"; a figure holding a cane (pilgrim) or a crook (if the figure is the Good Shepherd); to the right, a city (probably Jerusalem) and another construction to the left (possibly a temple); two swords and, in another part, a hand armed with a dagger (fig. 12A). What is at the center of the composition varies according to the representations, whereas the rest of the motifs remain the same. The *Ms Francken* displays a hand armed with a dagger (or a sword) at the right edge of the triangle, which corresponds to the degree of Elect; at the left point there are two swords and at the bottom a compass (fig. 12 c). These two swords should not be confused with the two black and white daggers, which were introduced into the rituals much more recently.

**The two swords**, which are also found on the collars of the "white" degrees (fig. 34), are mentioned in the *Gospel of Luke* (22:38): "*Domine, ecce duo gladii hic. At ille dixit eis: satis est.*" The motif is taken up by authors such as Giles of Rome (1247–1316), who wrote *On Ecclesiastical Power*, which was dedicated to the Supreme Pontiff during the quarrel between Boniface VIII and Philippe the Fair. The pontiff receives the two swords, which symbolize the two powers, spiritual and temporal, imperial (or royal) power and priestly power. The spiritual sword is to be used; the material sword is for the purposes of commanding. The two swords separate the reign of government, the *auctoritas* (power without effective execution) and *potestas* (exercisable power). God must be powerless for the world to be well governed.[10] The relationship between the blue degrees (obedience) at the moment they are "democratized" through election on the one hand, and on the other, the high degrees, the self-appointed "keepers" of the tradition and of its exegesis, are crucial for control of the Masonic domain. Paradoxically, it is the blue degrees (and thus the obediences) who need to "control" the rites entrusted to the high degrees, to establish their symbolic power. The example of the *Convent des Philalèthes*, studied by C. Porset, shows this type of control.[11] The convening of a convent in 1785 and 1787 at the invitation of the *Amis Réunis*, which brought together the various rites of the Masonic Enlightenment to define the nature and the reality of "Masonic science," allowed Savalette de Lange to symbolically legitimize the aim of the GODF to unify the "Masonic bodies." The Grand Orient therefore endeavored to control the high degrees via the secret structure of the Philalèthes, by setting the common corpus on behalf of the Grand Orient of France, which ensured its control of the situation, independently of any recognized legitimacy. The eighteenth century illustrated this struggle for symbolic power on three occasions. In all three cases, the high degrees (the *auctoritas*) faced the blue degrees (the *potestas*). The periodic resurgence of this struggle throughout Masonic history brings a smile in response to the traditionalist protestations of faith that are still convoked to support true or false takeovers. It also shows the "essential" importance, in the sense of a deep identity, of the microcosm in which it is the same actors who are at work in the "blue" side and in that of the high degrees. Their horizon of expectations is surreptitiously limited by the summit that legitimizes the system—that is, the *auctoritas*—and that states the *jus*. This is why the systems for high degrees value the appellation of "Jurisdictions" so highly.

It might be suggested, then, that the "Royal Secret" can be understood as an awareness of the void identified at the center of power—as it has been placed at the center of political thought in writers as varied as Agamben for prerevolutionary traditional societies and Lefort for contemporary democratic societies.[12]

## D. Jerusalem

The *Instruction* of the thirty-second degree asks:

D Where are you going?
R To the East
D Why?
R To enter into the legacy of my fathers

---

[10] Agamben, *The Kingdom and the Glory*, 167.

[11] Porset, *Les Philalèthes et les Convents de Paris. Une politique de la folie.*

[12] In Lefort, the disappearance of the body politic of the leader (such as the death of the king in Kantorowicz), makes the place of power, previously occupied by an eternal substance that transcends the simple physical existence of monarchs, an "empty place," which competing interest and opinion groups can succeed to one after the other, though only for a time and through elections.

D How can you enter?

R By the protection of the God of the armies and by the ascendancy that virtue will sooner or later gain.

Jerusalem is the aim of the initiatory journey, and it is here that one finds the operative dynamics of the labyrinth in cathedrals that is called "the path to Jerusalem" and that represents the aim to be achieved at its center (fig. 13). In the Middle Ages, navigating the labyrinth was both a symbol of and supplement to the pilgrimage to Jerusalem.

At the moment of breaking camp and forming the procession, the Grand Commander says: "And you, Young Knight, follow us to Jerusalem, where all the faithful guardians of the Sacred Treasure will soon gather." Here the "center of the center" is represented by the highest degrees of masonry, the *nec plus ultra*, which is both the innermost—since it is the most central, according to the analogy of the middle room for masters placed at the center of the lodge and responsible for collecting that which is scattered—and well placed at the end of the asymptotic pursuit of the inner self. The masters lead the works just as the Commander, placed at the center of the composition, leads the armies of the camp. When the elevation plan is drafted, as masters have learned to do since they were elevated to their own position, this central point becomes the highest one, the Zenith: the nodal point of the perpendicular that allows circulation between the top and bottom.[13]

Clearly, a quite different perspective on Jerusalem opens up, as the earthly Jerusalem—that of the Temple and the Ark of the Covenant that it preserves—corresponds to the heavenly Jerusalem, that of the Revelation of John, who, in his vision, of course incorporates the Four Living Creatures and thereby responds to Ezekiel's vision. When the drawing is raised one better grasps the instruction specified by the ritual with regard to the layout of the camp: "The Orient, which usually represents a glory [I will return to this essential motif], is one of the reception points replaced by the perspective of the city of Jerusalem." Gamble's lodge tracing board (1769, fig. 22), for the seventeenth degree of the AASR (which is devoted to the Apocalypse), namely the Knight of the East and the West, explicitly shows the Four Living Creatures. These preside over the opening of the seals. The first seal is indicated by the lion, the second by the ox, the third by the angel, and the fourth by the eagle. It should be noted—and this is no coincidence—that the tracing boards of the seventeenth degree are in a heptagon that is identical to the one contained in the thirty-second degree.[14] The same logic of center/periphery governs the economy of the iconography of the twenty-eighth degree (Knight of the Sun), which at its center shows the representation of the inner sun coinciding with the parabolic figuration of the Old Adam, substituted for that of the Good Shepherd, Hermes Kriophoros, or even Christ! This is why the cross is at the center of the representations of the Four Living Creatures: "By accepting that monastic practice is a 'translation' of Jewish ortho-

---

[13] Jardin, "Représentations du Centre," 53–83.

[14] Jardin, *Emprunts opératifs*, 2,144–147.

praxy, there is a perfect tropological consistency in painting Christ [the red cross on the tracing boards of the thirty-second degree] in the place reserved for Jerusalem."[15] And the tabernacle integrates the circle of the figures of the tetramorph.

## III - The Five Flags, or the Tetramorph, the Tabernacle, and Their Meaning.

*A. The Four Flags and the Tetramorph.*

The ritual explains the organization of the camp very precisely:

EXPLANATION OF THE CAMP
The corps formed by the meeting is commanded by five brave princes, who receive directly from the sovereign of sovereigns the order that they are to carry out. Their flags, designated by the letters T.E.N.G.U., are attached to the corners of the pentagon.

I suggest seeing a representation of the tetramorph (the Four Living Creatures) and the ark that they usually surround in the flags or standards of the five tents of the center of the camp. The lion, the bull, eagle, and the angel are the four figures that surround the fifth, through which the speech begins, and which is inserted into the circle rather than being at the center of the com-

position. For the center is reserved for what is in the Ark—that is, the triangle of the divine presence.

The animals certainly have meaning by themselves. Their representations are also very common in heraldry—especially those of the lion and the eagle. And many commentaries on the ceremonial speeches paraphrase them. However, their specific positioning in the iconographic field requires them to be related to one another and can perhaps reveal an esoteric secret of the degree, and even the Royal Secret itself. The tetramorph that brings together the four motifs from Ezekiel's vision is associated with the divine chariot and its wheels (fig. 14); it is also called "Four Living Creatures." We find it in John's vision in Revelations.

The motif is a most ancient one, and it spans the old and new testaments. Originally, the four animals were supposed to represent the four sons of Horus in the form of a bird, a fox, a monkey, and a man. Most probably Assyro-Babylonian cherubim, these animals are found on the lodge tracing boards of the Strict Observance and the "Scottish green" degree[16] (see infra). Beyond Ezekiel's vision, they are included in Christianity as the symbol of the evangelists according to the following associations:

- The man (with wings) corresponds to Matthew because the Gospel of Matthew starts with the presentation of Jesus's human genealogy.

---

[15] Carruthers, *Machina memorialis*, 293.

[16] The parallels between the Four Living Creatures and the symbol of the four sons of Horus in the form of the bird, the fox, the monkey, and the man, found on the tracing boards of the Strict Observance, is never suggested. It must be said that the ritual of the Marquis de Gages (1763–67) links the "four fundamental points of the tracing board" to "fineness, wisdom, speed, strength in all enterprises for the Order, represented by the emblem of the fox, the monkey, the hawk, and the lion."

- The lion corresponds to Mark in memory of the third verse of the gospel; "the voice of one crying in the wilderness."
- The ox is associated with Luke because his gospel begins with the sacrifice of Zechariah, father of John the Baptist.
- Finally, the eagle corresponds to John because from its prologue, his Gospel "transports the faithful to heaven."

Turning to the church fathers (Irenaeus, Origen, Eusebius, Jerome, Ambrose, Augustine, Pseudo-Dionysius, and Gregory[17]), medieval theologians explained that: "By birth, Jesus was a man (incarnation), by his death, he was an ox, slain and sacrificed (passion), by his resurrection he was a lion, and finally he was an eagle at the time of his ascension." In all cases, the animals of the tetramorph are the guardians of the path, and then of the tabernacle or the ark; the word *Ark* itself means "passage." It is for this reason that the doorways of Romanesque churches are designed to be like the gate of heaven, guarded by the Four Living Creatures.[18]

Let us look at how this tetramorph corresponds to the camp's flags.

1° the flag T, which is that of the Knights of the Sun, is azure, with a golden lion that is holding a golden key in its mouth and that has a golden collar on which the number 525 is engraved.[19]

At the top *Ad majorem dei gloriam* is written (fig. 21a, 21B, and 21 c).

The motto *Ad majorem dei gloriam* was originally used by Ignatius of Loyola before becoming that of the Jesuits.

The lion is identical to the lion of the tetramorph here. The lion, the most used animal in medieval heraldry, evokes strength and courage, but also Christ, "perhaps owing to its supposed power to resurrect stillborn cubs with its breath."[20] In coats of arms the lion is always seen in profile. On the different seals of the thirty-second degree, it is represented lying or leaping, which in fact corresponds to later (post-medieval) representations. In the earliest depictions of the camp, the lion holds the golden key in its mouth, the presence of which must be explained. The legend of the Royal Arch, introduced at the thirteenth degree of the Rite of Perfection (or the Royal Secret), makes the Grand Treasurer, who represents Guibelum, the keeper of the "sacred treasure of the Masons"—that is, he carries out the mission later entrusted to the Sublime Prince of the

---

[17] References to the texts and a quick analysis of them can all be found in Fromaget, *Le symbolisme des quatre Vivants*, 61–69.

[18] For a precise study of the Four Living Creatures, see M. Fromaget, *Le symbolisme des quatre Vivants*.

[19] The number 525 can be linked to 515, the number used by Dante in *The Divine Comedy* (Purgatory XXXIII, 43–44); Without putting forward anything solid, Guénon noted (for many reasons, the historian must always be wary of Guénon!) that it is the opposite number to 666, the number of the beast, and that it "corresponds to the general design of the Empire according to Dante" (see Guénon, *L'Ésotérisme de Dante*, 74–77).

[20] Guénon, *L'Ésotérisme de Dante*, 136.

Royal Secret. He carries "a small key" and "the letters I, V, IOL, which are the initials of *Inveni Verbum in Ore Leonis*."[21] The degree brings in the lion and the key in the following manner:

> The Ark of the Covenant was lost in a forest and then recovered through the roar of a lion, which ceased roaring and lay down upon the approach of the Israelites. This lion had previously devoured . . . many Egyptians who attempted to take the Ark; he kept in his mouth the key of the Ark, and upon the approach of the High Priest he dropped it and . . . lay as though tamed.[22]

The lion, in addition to its classical solar and royal functions, becomes here the keeper of the most precious treasure, the Ark, and, beyond this Ark, keeper of the Word. I should recall here the exact title of the ritual that I am using: *Knight of Saint Andrew, Faithful **Keeper of the Sacred Treasure** and Valiant Prince of the Royal Secret*. Also worth noting is the importance of the degree of Royal Arch, confirmed by the following flag, as a connecting degree between the iconography of the Antients and that of the thirty-second degree of the AASR, which I will examine below.

2 ° Flag E is that of the Royal Arch. It is silver and has a blazing heart supported by two (striped vert) sable wings and crowned with a vert laurel.

Flag E represents the angel or man of the tetramorph. The silver tincture is effectively represented by "white," but if the wings are sable they would be black (a reference to the Knight of the Black Eagle, perhaps) and not golden, as shown in the tracing board in the Meyer collection (fig. 21a, 21B and 21 c). I have discovered what seems to me to be the first, very early occurrence of the exact motif of the crowned and winged heart that appears on the flag. It is on the lodge tracing board "La loge physique de Chevalier du soleil" of the *atlas Loiven* (fig. 26 and 26A). On this tracing board the motif of the winged heart represents the Spirit (*spiritus*), associated with the *corpus* and the *anima*.

3 ° Flag N, which belongs to the Grand Master of the Key, is sea green and features a consummate outstretched, fierce eagle.

This flag represents the eagle of the tetramorph. The "sea green" should be called "vert." The outstretched eagle has two crowned heads, and it holds in its talons the heart and the sword. We can see the first iconographic representation of the eagle on the lodge tracing board of the Knight of the Black Eagle for the ritual from *La maçonnerie des hommes*, kept in the Hague (fig. 27 and 27A).

4° Flag G, that of the Patriarchs, is golden and features a sable [= black] ox.

---

[21] *Ms Francken de 1783*, Lamoine translation, 83. This quotation and of the following one were found by C. Guérillot, *La Rose maçonnique*, 2, 106. [Translator's note: Quotation back-translated from the French-language version of this article.]

[22] *Ms Francken de 1783*, Lamoine translation, 87. [Translator's note: Quotation back-translated from the French-language version of this article.]

The ox and the bull are distinguished from the seventeenth century in the following way; "The ox has its tail between its legs, while the bull's is erect and curls toward its back."[23] In accordance with these codes, what we have here is an ox! I have not yet found any ancient Masonic representation of the motif.

5° Finally, flag U (or that of the Great Pontiffs) is purpure [=purple] and features the Ark of the Covenant between two burning torches and topped with two hooped palms.

Above the arch *Laus Deo* is written.

The ark traditionally placed at the center of the tetramorph is associated here, in flag form, with the circle of the Four Living Creatures. Nevertheless, it remains at the heart of the system that it oversees through its position "on top" of the composition, much like on the coat of arms of Antients (see below). The representation of the Ark is borrowed from multiple Masonic occurrences of the motif (since the one in the *Parfait Maçon*, 1744, for example), which were themselves borrowed from different eighteenth-century bibles and the illustrations of Flavius Josephus's *Antiquities of the Jews*.

The quasi-systematic presence of the heart on the flags should be noted. There is one in the talons of the eagle; there is a winged heart; there is one held by the lion in the tracing board of the Meyer collection; and there is perhaps one over the Ark on the Douai tracing board. We know from Jeremiah (Jer. 32, 33) that Yahweh will write his word in the very heart of man, but

this theme, echoed by Ezekiel ("And I will give them one heart, and I will put a new spirit within you; and I will take the stony heart out of their flesh, and will give them an heart of flesh" (Ez. 11: 19–20)), spans all of Masonry, from the compass point placed on the heart during the first initiation. Masons know that, lacking their land, they must rebuild the temple in their hearts.

The tetramorph, which is a frequent presence in Romanesque art, especially on the tympana of doorways (fig. 16), underwent a relative decline in parallel to that of the theological commentaries on the motif. The tetramorph also appears in Masonic iconography, in particular on the coat of arms of the Antients (or Ancients) and the lodge tracing boards of the Strict Observance, where it flanks Hiram's tomb (figs. 17 and 20) and in fact transforms it into an Ark. This is consistent because the tomb, as demonstrated by the degree of Perfect Master (fifth degree of the AASR), would henceforth house the Name, engraved on the delta of the coffin.

However, some attributes change or are complemented by a specifically Masonic symbolism. The representation of the lion is stable, though it receives a gold key; the eagle (a hawk in Larudan's revelations), receives a golden crown at the thirty-second degree; the man or angel acts the beast by taking the form of a monkey in Larudan (though in this exact case to become Thoth/Hermes (fig. 19) while on the tracing board of the thirty-second degree, he becomes a winged heart (fig. 21). The ox becomes a fox in Larudan, and returns to being an ox on the tracing board of the Sovereign Prince of the Royal Secret.

---

[23] Pastoureau, *Traité d'héraldique*, 147.

Another level of analysis is necessary because the camp of the thirty-second degree seems to make explicit reference to the Hebrew camp established in the desert (fig. 25). In the Bible, Numbers 1 specifies the organization of the camp:

Yahweh . . . said: The sons of Israel are to pitch their tents, every man by his own standard, under the banner of his patriarchal House. They are to pitch their tents all around the tabernacle of the Testimony, at a measured distance. Those who are to pitch their tents on the east side: Toward the sunrise, the standard of the camp of Judah. . . . On the south side, the standard of the camp of Reuben. . . . Next the Tent of Meeting will move, since the camp of the Levites is situated in the middle of the other camps. The order of movement is to be the order of encampment, every man under his own standard. . . . On the west side, the standard of the camp of Ephraim. . . . On the north side, the standard of the camp of Dan . . . The sons of Israel did exactly as Yahweh had ordered Moses. This was how they pitched camp, grouped by standards.[24]

This arrangement of the twelve tribes "grouped in a square, three by three at each point, would survive in the plan of the ideal temple designed by Ezekiel, and then finally in the heavenly Jerusalem. . . . It appears as a watermark, reduced to its simplest expression, in the form of the Four Living Creatures."[25]

The *Targum Pseudo-Jonathan* says that the emblems are those of the tetramorph: the lion for the tribes of Judah, Issachar, and Zebulun; man for those of Reuben, Simeon, and Gad (fig. 24); the bull for those of Ephraim, Manasseh, and Benjamin; and finally the eagle for those of Dan, Asher, and Napthali.[26] The standards of the twelve tribes bear as emblems the animals or objects with which Jacob identifies his sons when he blesses them shortly before his death. According to Exodus (28:21), the color of each tribe's banner matches that of the precious stones that make up the breastplate of Aaron. The banner of the tribe of Judah is therefore sky blue, the color of carbuncle, and it bears the lion; that of Ruben is red, the color of ruby, and it bears the emblem of mandrakes or man; that of Ephraim is black, the color of onyx and jet. A young ox appears on the flag of Ephraim, and a wild ox is on the flag of Manasseh. Finally, Dan's stone is the jacinth, but the animal associated with him in the classifications of the twelve tribes is the snake and not the eagle. Moreover, "in the Jewish tradition each of the four creatures corresponds to the four letters of the divine name YHVH: Y for man, H for lion, V for bull, and the second H for eagle."[27]

---

[24] Jones, ed., *The Jerusalem Bible: Reader's Edition*, 143–144.

[25] De Champeaux, *Introduction au monde des symboles*, 429.

[26] De Champeaux, *Introduction au monde des symboles*, 429.

[27] De Champeaux, *Introduction au monde des symboles*, 429.

## B. *The Fifth Flag, the Ark or the Tabernacle*

The ark motif is commonplace in the Masonic iconography that is found on many lodge tracing boards. During the seventeenth and eighteenth centuries, it was borrowed from the bibles as well as editions of Flavius Josephus's histories of the Jews. In the scale of degrees, the Ark would very quickly be surrounded by two palm trees, which are a vegetable version of the wings of the cherubim that cover and care for it.

Carruthers has shown how the tabernacle, which houses the word of God, is a medium for medieval monastic meditation and how its description is in fact a prescription.[28] Going back long before the Renaissance authors studied by Yates in her *Art of Memory*, the author shows how Albert the Great based "the paradigm of the architectural mnemonic" on monasteries by building not a real object but a fictional one for the purposes of meditation: "There is an analogy between the idea that the Temple is a 'way' and the use of mandalas in Buddhist meditation. . . . These symbols have an initiatory value." She recalls how, in the Middle Ages, there was a transition, through "rhetorical plays on words," from a "treasure chest of memory to the treasure chest that is the Ark of Moses."[29] She then describes "the chain of associations that leads from the chest (*arca*) in which the precious law . . . is concealed—that is, the treasure chest of memory."[30] Of course, these keys to understanding bring us very close to the Royal Secret, and/or the treasure, entrusted to the custody of the Valiant and Sublime Princes of the Royal Secret!

The importance of the tabernacle is also attested by the place reserved for its maker, Bezalel. "So much did Bezalel of the tribe of Judah please God that He filled him with his spirit to work on the construction of the tabernacle and the things necessary for divine worship Ex. 31:2," which is the explanation offered by the ritual of the thirty-second degree in the note accompanying the name BEZALEL, Commander of the second army corps.

The first Masonic texts, all too often forgotten, must of course be made use of to grasp the keys they offer. Accordingly, Bezalel, the constructor of the Ark, is the prototype of Solomon, who ordered the construction of the temple and, furthermore, that of Hiram the Builder. Bezalel is the great nephew of Moses, who is charged by Moses with building the tabernacle.

> The two younger brothers of the fforesaid king alboyin disired for to be instructed by him [Bezalel] his noble asiance by which he wrought to which he agreed conditionally they were not to discover it without a another to themselves to make a trible voice so they entered oath and he tought them the heorick and the practick part of masonry.[31]

---

[28] Carruthers, *Machina memorialis*, see especially chapter 5, "Le lieu du tabernacle," 279–342.

[29] Carruthers, *Machina memorialis*, 306. [Translator's note: Quotation back-translated from the French-language version of this article.]

[30] Carruthers, *Machina memorialis*, 336. [Translator's note: Quotation back-translated from the French-language version of this article.]

[31] *Ms Graham*, 1726.

Later in the text, Bezalel the builder wished to be buried in the Valley of Jehoshaphat, and as with that of Phaleg, his tomb is engraved with an epitaph.

> this was cutte as follows—Here Lys the flowr o masonry superiour of many other companion to a king and two princes a brothe Here Lys the heart all secrets could conceal Here lys the tongue that never did reveal —now after his death the inhabitance there about did think that the secrets of masonry had been totally Lost . . . yet it is to be beleiued and allso under stood that such a holy secret could never be Lost while any good servant of God remained alive on the earth for every good servant of God had hath and allways will have a great part of that holy secret alltho they know it not themselves . . . they were Seeking ffor what they did no want But their deep Ignorance could not disarne it..[32]

What is striking, as Horne underscores, "is that at the very time when it is generally accepted that the legend of Hiram began to be adopted and to circulate in the English speculative process, we have clear proof, even if it comes from the North of England, that an almost identical story was told about Noah." On this point Horne explains:

> The *Ms Graham* offers many symbolic allusions, ideas, and practices about the period in question, and associated with the noachite legend itself, another legend comes immediately after, linked to Bezalel, constructor of the Tabernacle of Moses in the desert."[33]

Horne therefore shows the obvious link between the constructor of an Ark (Noah) and a subsequent builder of a resting place for the Ark (Solomon). He continues:

> It is perhaps also significant that the history of the construction of King Solomon's temple, as given to us by the Old Charges since *Ms Cooke*, comes immediately after these stories of Bezalel and Noah, while elements of the three stories are now collapsed into one in our current legend.

Note that, step by step, the camp of the twelve tribes is animated and set in motion according to a circular order that begins with the Orient: this is the direction of the sun that rises and gives life to the Earth. The armies of the camp in the thirty-second degree mobilize starting with Ezra, and then, the ritual specifies,

> According to their rank the eight other heads of the nonagon. After these the leaders of the pentagon, and then the Knights Kadosh, the Knights of Malta, and the Princes of the Royal secret. After these come the recipient, the Master of Ceremonies, and the preparer, and the march is completed by the principal dignitaries of the Consistory, the two lieutenants and the Sovereign Grand Commander.

---

[32] *Ms Graham*, 1726. See also Rousse Lacordaire, *Jésus dans la tradition maçonnique*, 70–71.

[33] Horne, *Le Temple de Salomon dans la tradition maçonnique*. [Translator's note: Quotation back-translated from the French-language version of this article.]

The "protocolary" order of entry into the lodge order is respected here and does not at all correspond to the "biblical" logic. The camp of the thirty-second degree comes into life from the outskirts so that the last Masons to set off are those who are placed in the center of the triangle. The procession therefore arranges a movement in which everyone is located precisely in a mnemonic place. We have also seen how the wind that blows the flags determines the movement of the letters TENGU, SALIX NONI in the opposite direction to the path of the sun, as if it were necessary to deconstruct the word or even the way in which the steps, in the oldest rituals, are undone by a step backward.

## C. The Tetramorph and Iconography of the Antients

It is worth highlighting how the central motif of the camp of the thirty-second degree is a transposition of the central motif of the arms of the Ancients, which also display the Four Living Creatures. The heraldry and iconography here provide another obvious parallel and guide us: Dermott's 1756 work *Ahiman Rezon* (fig. 28 a) contains the coat of arms of the Ancients (fig. 28 b). It would be worth expanding the horizons of inquiry at this point and examining why and how the Ancients (or Antients) borrowed the medieval motif of the tetramorph and what texts are associated with this loan. The "Kirkwall Scroll" of Lodge Kirkwall Kilwinning in Scotland shows the first Masonic occurrence of the motif (fig. 29). It should also be noted that the *Ahiman Rezon* offers four prayers that bear a resemblance to the five prayers made before each of the cities during the peregrination of the Sublime Princes of the Royal Secret.

-The Royal Arch has the flags of the twelve tribes of Israel but also those of each of the Four Living Creatures (fig. 30 and 30a). The fourteenth degree of Francken's Rite of Perfection entrusts the inspection of each of the tribes of Israel to the twelve Master Elects, whose names are given.[34] These tribes are represented in Barker's Bible of 1599.

- Although the camp of the thirty-second degree of the AASR places the flags of the Four Living Creatures at its heart, it is of course inconceivable that the creators and writers of the degree and the tracing board would have been unaware of the prominent and central place of the motif on the coat of arms of the Antients, particularly as it is topped by the Ark! Did this motif become an archetype that facilitated the crystallization of influences and the mobilization of a group of Masons in the construction of a "summit" degree? What can be taken from these parallels if not a striking variation of the motifs that seems to link the Masonry of the Antients to the Sublime Prince of Royal Secret of the AASR via a "British" Royal Arch that has not been kept as such by the construction of this same AASR? At any rate, the easily identifiable and by all accounts explicit "migration of symbols" via iconography allows questions to be asked.

---

[34] *Ms Francken*, 1783.

[35] Lévy, *Quelques moments de l'histoire du REAA*, Chapter 4.

J-B. Lévy[35] asks whether the AASR is Modern or Antient. And in the debate on the respective place of the two influences, he comes down on the side of the Moderns and puts forward the chronological argument that "the AASR comes from the Rite of the Royal Secret, developed by Morin and Francken from rituals that Morin took from France at a time when the only known Rite was that of the Moderns." He further notes that: "Almost all of the degrees from the fourth to the thirty-third originate from degrees practiced in France before the arrival of the Rite of the *Antients*." The debate, which has long focused on the first three degrees from the book *Les trois coups distincts* (1760) and from the *Guide des maçons écossais*, can be transposed to the high degrees by substituting chronological issues for motif-based ones. Although it is impossible to speak with real certainty, it is possible to identify what seems to be the influence of a major theme (to which Trinitarian traces could be added) of the Antients on the construction of the degree.

The positioning of the Four Living Creatures in the tracing board of the Lodge of the Strict Observance (fig. 17) and in some Scottish tracing boards (fig. 18)—which in this case have Germanic influences—should also be noted. This presence of the Four Living Creatures transforms the tomb that houses the Delta, carrying the name of God on the casket of Hiram, in the form of an Ark.

A more comprehensive question leads one to query the presence of the tetramorph in Masonry in view of the fact that the motif has practically been retired in the theological domain (its hour of glory came with Romanesque art!). It seems that we have here a new illustration of the ability of Masonic symbolism to "recycle" based on complex lineaments and "obsolete" symbols from other areas, doing so according to a logic of the esoteric construction of a tradition.

## D. The Heptagon and the Nonagon

The heptagon is "empty" of motifs, but it important to keep in mind its matrix role in lodge tracing boards for the seventeenth degree (mentioned above), which are contained within a heptagon that corresponds to Revelation and thus also, in a certain way, to the Four Living Creatures.

The ritual says:

The nonagon that the outline of the tracing board forms designates [designates repeated] the placement in the army occupied by the Princes of Jerusalem, the Knights of the East and the West, the Knights R+, and all other Masons of a rank lower than these, whose leaders receive the orders of the five Princes of the Pentagon and are divided into nine camps that are designated by a tent.

S Tent S, named MALACHIAS, is that of the Knights of R+, the Knights of the East and the West, and the Princes of Jerusalem. The flag or pennon that distinguishes it is a white that is tinted with red [= gules]

A The sea-green pennon [= vert] that can be seen on tent A, named ZERUBBABEL, represents the camp of the Knights of the Sword.

---

[35] Lévy, *Quelques moments de l'histoire du REAA*, Chapter 4.

Sea green is the color of the degree of Knight of the Sword, since Zerubbabel passes through a sea-green river; in the Middle Ages green represented water.

L  The pennon of tent L, called NE-HEMIAS, is that of the Great Elect Sublime Masons, and its color is red [= gules].

I  Tent I, called HOBEN, represents the camp of the Great Architects and the Knights of the Royal Arch. Its pennon is red and black. [= gules and sable]

S  Tent S, named PHALEG, is that of the sublime and illustrious Elected of 9 and 15. Its pennon is black. [= sable]

The two pennons are reversed on the seal of the Meyer collection.

N  Tent N, known by the name of JE-HOIADA, refers to the camp of the Provosts and Judges. Its pennon is diamonds of gules and sable.

O  Tent O, named ABDA, is that of the Intendants of the Buildings or Intimate Secretaries. Its pennon is gules and vert.

N  Tent N. known as JOSHUA, with a green [= vert] flag or pennon, represents the camp of the Secret or Perfect Masters.

I  Finally, tent I, named EZRA, is that of symbolic and voluntary Masters. Its pennon is blue. [= azure]

It is noticeable the extent to which heraldic language, which is extensively used to describe the flags, is practically abandoned to describe the pennons. However, it is worth remarking that blazonry rules are respected. We should note that on the tracing board of the Meyer collection, the colors of the pennons are repeated in the circle in the central triangle (fig. 6). Once verified, there would be no change in the "heraldic coding" offered by the various rituals of

the eighteenth century. On the other hand, there is a mixture of heraldic and common vocabulary: thus blue is sometimes called blue, and sometimes azure, green is sometimes called green, and sometimes vert, and so on. This is the case regardless of the ritual.

The colors are not randomly distributed (fig 5 a.). Blue (azure) corresponds to the Masters who represent blue masonry; green (vert) is conferred on the Scottish (chronologically the first Scottish are the "green Scottish" who would give their color to the degree of Perfect Master, as shown in the iconography of the lodge degree tracing boards). If we take as a reference the ritual *Kloss XXVII*, circa 1804, we find that the colors often (though not always) match those of the lodge decor for the different degrees. We therefore find the following correspondences—in the very real sense of the term and also in a heraldic context—of colors:

- The tribes assembled at the camp around "the tent of the desert"
- The stones of Aaron's breastplate
- The Four Living Creatures of Ezekiel's vision
- The Four Living Creatures of the evangelists
- The Four Living Creatures in John's Revelation
- Masonic degrees grouped by colors

Due to a lack of space, I cannot elaborate here on the correspondences established by Saints Maximus and Theophanes during the seventh and eighth centuries between the Four Living Creatures and the four elements of the alchemical process. This dimension also underpins the borrowings of the iconography of the camp of the thirty-second degree, based around the precise chosen representations: the black eagle with two crowned heads, which holds the bloodied heart and the sword in its claws, for example, is completely alchemical and deserves a separate study. The winged heart "borrowed" from the "physical lodge of the Knight of the Sun" introduces a new approach to the theme of "body, soul, spirit" previously articulated in the twenty-eighth degree.[36]

## V - Glory and the Royal Secret

### A. The Motif of Glory

The motif of the glory of God, which is particularly strong in the religious iconography of the Catholic counter-reformation, is explicit in the legends of the two flags that bear *Laus Deo* and *Ad majorem dei gloriam*. This dedication is especially used by the Jesuits.

The iconographic representation of the older tracing boards is characterized by the glories that radiate from the center to the periphery. The main motif of the innumerable rays that emanate from each geometric figure of the tracing board appears for the first time, and with great vigor, in the iconography of the *Ms Baylot*'s tracing board of the Prince of the Royal Secret (fig. 1). These rays are found—golden, as is proper—on the collars of the white degrees in two forms: from the central triangle of the collar and also the collar itself. The center circle itself radiates to fill the entire triangle. The triangle radiates in turn to the pentagram, which itself launches its rays toward the heptagram. Finally, the enneagram in turn radiates. These edges (fig. 6) are the symbol of glory. Decorators call these motifs "glory" or "great glory." This notion has a use

that is certainly symbolic, although it is also and especially political in the management of "Masonic salvation goods." The Royal Secret of the thirty-second degree is therefore at the interface of theology and politics; to understand this, it is necessary to grasp the keys offered by Agamben in his book *The Kingdom and the Glory*.[37]

According to this author, glory is the very specific place where the bilateral nature of the relationship between theology and politics appears and allows communication between their two roles. The weight of glory is particularly strong in the "white" degrees, where it appears explicitly on the collars in the form of rays that radiate from the triangle, which once more is the central motif.

Agamben asks: What is the relationship that so closely unites power and glory? Without having attended all the entry ceremonials of Masonic delegations, it is a question he sees as all the more pertinent because "ceremonial glory is frequently experienced by someone who receives it as a painful obligation." This is why all Masonic dignitaries protest their commitment to simplicity while reproducing in forms that are rarely divested of their significance the procession ceremony where the steel vault is a metaphor for the triumphal arch. Under these circumstances, the exchange of affectionate words and most fraternal greetings given to the Orient, together with the difficult exercise of the repetition of each glorious title, is not just a rhetoric of mutual reassurance and a communal culture that inducts the other (most often the new "president" of the lodge) into this community. It is also the absolute power of the ritual to produce glory,

---

[36] See Jardin, Voyages dans les tableaux de loges, 219–241.

[37] Agamben, *The Kingdom and the Glory*.

with a political functionality that we must examine. As with the arrangement of any procession, the procession ceremony of the armies of the camp of the thirty-second degree "produces" the glory.

In his book, Agamben recalls how, according to Schmitt, the significant concepts of the modern doctrine of the state are secularized theological concepts. I propose to build on his analyses to study the original connection between the Royal Art of governing—which is of interest to the "white" degrees and to the degree of the Royal Secret in particular—and the "Judaic creation" of political theology.[38]

## B. Glory, Royal Art, and Royal Secret

Israel is a theocracy, but according to Peterson,[39] in the Middle Ages, the theological-political paradigm of divine monarchy came into conflict with Trinitarian theology, which founded a form of politics based around participation in the glorious worship of angels and saints: "politics . . . is nothing else than the cultural anticipation of eschatological glory."[40] Accordingly, angelology works in a similar manner to the theological paradigm of administration;[41] there is a correspondence between the angels and officials, Agamben argues. This is why "the king reigns but does not govern." The administrative apparatus through which the king retains his kingdom in turn becomes the paradigm of the divine government of the world.[42] In chapter 6 of *Adversus Praxean*,[43] Tertullian suggests that the way in which "the stars and the whole heaven always move, and the sun" through God's signal determines a harmony that allows the universe to be called a *cosmos*, a word that means "order" (see fig. 12). The famous formula of *rex regnat, sed non gubernat*, which Schmitt traces back to the seventeenth-century polemics against King Sigismund III of Poland, may thus be the modern version of the Royal Secret. The distinction between reigning and governing overlaps with the distinction between *auctoritas* and *potestas*—and the one between high degrees (in particular white ones) and blue ones.[44] As Foucault later would, Schmitt sees the pastorate of the Catholic Church, which would be put in place in the seventeenth century, as "the paradigm of the modern concept of government." I cannot but emphasize here the proximity of the following degrees:

- on the one hand, the Knight of the Sun, centered on the figure of the Good Shepherd, who is by definition responsible for the pastoral

---

[38] Agamben, *The Kingdom and the Glory*, 9.

[39] Erik Peterson. *Ausgewiihlte Schriften*, vol. 1, *Theologische Traktate* (Würzburg: Echter, 1994), quoted in Agamben, *The Kingdom and the Glory*, 8–10.

[40] Agamben, *The Kingdom and the Glory*, 16.

[41] Agamben, *The Kingdom and the Glory*, 77.

[42] Agamben, *The Kingdom and the Glory*, 120.

[43] Quoted in Agamben, *The Kingdom and the Glory*, 72.

[44] See the third part of Jardin's thesis.

care that serves as the model for state governance from the seventeenth century, as Foucault has shown;[45]

• and on the other hand the Sublime Prince of the Royal Secret, if this secret concerns the Royal Art understood as the art of governing men.

*C. From the Army of Angels to the Army Corps of the Masons: Hymns of Glory, Acclamations, and Processions*

Agamben flushes out the distinction between two gods in Numenius, a second-century Neoplatonist writer. The one called "king" is transcendent and an outsider to the world. The other, the son of the former, is active, immanent to the world and governs it; he is bad. Agamben identifies in Thomas Aquinas the idea of the *Ordo* of the world, as a relationship both between creatures and God and between creatures themselves. Aquinas, similar to the camp of the thirty-second degree of the AASR, uses the metaphor of an army (armies were traditionally ordered into camps from antiquity, with medieval representations drawing attention to their tents and their flags, as well as their banners (fig. 7A):

Some order must be found in the parts of the universe; and so the universe has both aseparate good and a good of order. We see this, for example, in the case of an army.[46]

God in his very being is *ordo*, or order. The *dispositio* of things in the order means nothing else than the *dispositio* of things in God.

Peterson's thesis emphasizes the politico-religious character of the Church: "The cult of the celestial Church and, therefore, also the liturgy of the early Church that is bound to the celestial, have an originary relation with the world of politics." The song of praise and glory (see the Trisagion: *Sanctus, Sanctus, Sanctus*), originally means the angels, cherubim, and seraphim. This acclamation is included explicitly in the Morin ritual for the thirty-second degree through the form of *Laus Deo* (which equally explicitly includes the formula associated through the iconography with the tabernacle or with the Ark; fig. 5 a), repeated three times at the opening of the consistory and five times in the form of the *Amen* at the end of the recipient's Obligation.

To fully understand this liturgy, it is worth returning to the substitution carried out by the first Trinitarian Masonic rituals between angels and the Scottish, English, and Irish, something shown on a remarkable page of *Ms Brigon*. This *Manuscrit d'Ecossais trinitaire de Pirlet*, dated December 3, 1765 (C. Gagne collection),[47] features (fig. 31) the extraordinary sight of the words cherubim, seraphim, and archangels struck out and replaced with the words English, Scottish, and Architects! The heavenly army of angels is transmuted into a terrestrial

---

[45] Foucault, *Sécurité, territoire, population.*

[46] Thomas Aquinas, *Commentary on the Metaphysics of Aristotle,  12.12.2629–2630,* quoted in Agamben, *The Kingdom and the Glory,* 140.

[47] I would particularly like to thank Claude Gagne for his great kindness in allowing me to reproduce this manuscript excerpt.

army of high-degree Masons. The angels are in a hierarchy based on ranks, while the ecclesiastical (terrestrial) hierarchies are angelized, the word *hierarchia* meaning, according to Aquinas, "sacred power." Dionysius the Areopagite explains that "What is sacred and divine is hierarchically ordered, and its barely disguised strategy aims—through the obsessive repetition of a triadic schema that descends from the Trinity, via the angelic triarchies, to the earthly hierarchy—at the sacralization of power."[48] Agamben emphasizes that this is why the vocabulary of administration was first constructed in the sphere of angelology and corresponds to it. This substitution of armies of Masons for celestial armies of angels may seem preposterous to the secular Mason of the twenty-first century, but it probably did not to his eighteenth-century brother. The angels have certainly disappeared from rituals (the figure of the guardian angel appeared in the seventeenth century), but they have not from the iconography of lodge tracing boards, and we see the choir of angels surround the delta radiating glory on the Trinitarian tracing boards (fig. 32), or the cross on the Sovereign Prince Rose-Croix tracing boards (fig. 33), exactly on the model of molds for the Host from the eighteenth century (fig. 34). Deep into the structure, we therefore seem to have the first circle of five flags as a substitute for the tetramorph, though the latter remains explicit, and in the second circle the procession of the Masonic army corps in place of the heavenly angels. The two circles surround the delta (triangle) and the cross like a crown.

The historian Kantorowicz has shown how the political theology of the Carolingians developed, starting with Pepin the Short, as a restoration of biblical kingship against the Roman Empire and culminated in the introduction of the equally biblical rite of royal anointment, which made the latter sacred: the Carolingians performed a "liturgization" of secular power. This is the context into which the *Laudes regiae*, which simultaneously ordered the world's secular and ecclesiastical authorities and their celestial intercessors, must be repositioned. Henceforth the Church's recognition of new kings superseded the assent of the people, expressed through acclamations. The acclamation that "made" the sovereign was accompanied by the gesture of raising the right hand, or by applause, with wishes of strength, prayer, victory, or life (vivas), for example the clapping that accompanies the *Vivat* of the French Rite or just simply the "warm rounds" of applause during the election of a president of the lodge.

At the coronation of Charlemagne in 800, the song of praise implied that "the new king was acclaimed also by the choirs of angels and saints, as well as by Christ himself, who, in his quality as Victor, King, and Commander, recognized the new christus of the Church as his fellow ruler."[49] Agamben links the seemingly contradictory theses of Schmitt, according to whom "all significant concepts of the modern theory of the state are secularized theological concepts," and Assmann, who turns that view on its head in suggesting that "the significant concepts of theology are theologized political concepts."

---

[48] Agamben, *The Kingdom and the Glory*, 153.

[49] Agamben, *The Kingdom and the Glory*, 190–191.

The "glory to God" is defined by Maimonides in *The Guide for the Perplexed*: "*Kabhod* or 'Glory to the Lord', signifies the created light that God sends down on a specific place. . . . Praise is called *kabhod* (glory)."

Agamben explains that:

1) Glory is a devouring fire;

2) The term refers to the essence of God; the *Kabhod* is blinding and a veil must protect Moses's eyes when he speaks to God.

The *Kabhod*, as created light, conceals the *Kabhod* as the essence or true being of God.

3) The third meaning is that of praise. According to Rabbinic tradition, the *kabhod YHWH* is linked with the *Shekinah*, which expresses the presence of God among men.[50] Agamben points out the circularity of the economy of salvation; Jesus fulfilled the glorification of the Father (economy of glory) and at the same time the glorification of the Son by the Father; the Son is therefore the reflection and radiance of the glory of God.[51] We therefore have a Trinitarian logic here. There is another Christian meaning in the initiatory concerns of Masons, namely "transfiguration." In his bright mandorla of glory, the Christ of the Romanesque doorways, surrounded by the tetramorph, is transformed into a "spiritual or glorious" body, as he was on Mount Tabor. This signifies that the Four Living Creatures indicate the passage from earthly form to "divine" status, from the West to the East.

The acclamation of "thrice holy" with which the seraphim (but also the cherubim, therefore the Four Living Creatures[52]), sing the glory of God in heaven, the troops and the armies of angels and archangels for the service of the glory of God, are justified by the formula: "For unto Thee is due all glory." Glory is the attribute not of government but of reigning. However, "the center of the machine is empty, and glory is nothing but the splendor that emanates from this emptiness, the inexhaustible *kabhod* that at once reveals and veils the central vacuity of the machine."[53] The Four Living Creatures of course of course play an important role in the heavenly liturgy that is described as follows in John's Revelation:

> And they do not rest day or night, saying: "Holy, holy, holy, the Lord God Almighty, Who was and is and is to come!" Whenever the living creatures give glory and honor and thanks to Him who sits on the throne . . . the twenty-four elders fall down before Him."[54]

Of course, the structure of the heavenly Jerusalem described by Revelation is prefigured by the square arrangement of the camp established in the desert by the twelve tribes of Israel, dictated by God to Moses.

---

[50] Agamben, *The Kingdom and the Glory*, 200.

[51] Pages 312–335 (French-language version) of Agamben's work develop some very interesting considerations on glory, strength, and beauty.

[52] See Fromaget, *Le Symbolisme des quatre vivants*, 43–44.

[53] Agamben, *The Kingdom and the Glory*, 211.

[54] Revelations 4:8.

*Amen* is another acclamation that became a simple formula for ending a prayer in the fourth century. The *Talmud* (b Shab., 119 b), states: "The gates of paradise shall be opened to he who replies Amen with all of his might."[55] The acclamation of "Amen" is explicitly repeated five times following the end of the Obligation in the ritual of the thirty-second degree: "May God keep me in my duties to justice and equity. *Amen, Amen, Amen, Amen, Amen, Amen.*" Then, systematically, five times also, it is repeated at the end of each prayer before each port and during the incense ceremony that immediately precedes the closing of the works.

Agamben poses the key question: "How does the liturgy 'make' power? If the governmental machine is twofold (Kingdom and Government), what function does glory play within it?"[56] He also brings up the problem posed by Augustine relating to the inoperativity of the blessed after the Last Judgment, and resolves it brilliantly: "Glory, both in theology and in politics, is precisely what takes the place of that unthinkable emptiness that amounts to the inoperativity of power."[57] This emptiness of power finds its iconographic symbol in the image of the empty throne, of which he offers multiple occurrences. The throne of YHWH was created before the creation of the world, and it is the symbol not of royalty, but of glory.[58]

The real problem, as Agamben notes, is not sovereignty but government; it is not God but the angel; it is not the king but the minister. The concept of order plays a major role here. Providential order—the *ordo* that influences the physiocrats—is the very being of God, the founder of the government of the world. According to Leibnitz, Spinoza merely promoted these theses. "The divine government of the world is so absolute and it penetrates creatures so deeply, that the divine will is annulled in the freedom of men (and the latter in the former)." Agamben emphasizes: "At this point, theology can resolve itself into atheism, and providentialism into democracy, because God has made the world just as if it were without God and governs it as though it governed itself." Agamben completes his work by citing Bossuet's *Traité du libre arbitre* (2, chap. 8, 64), in which Bossuet identifies the world created by God in the world without God. And he concludes: "Modernity, removing God from the world, has not only failed to leave theology behind, but in some ways has done nothing other than to lead the project of the providential oikonomia to completion."[59]

By pointing out the appropriation of very ancient motifs such as the tetramorph, and perhaps precisely via an "underground" transmission by the Antients, the iconographic study of the tracing board of the camp of the thirty-second degree allows us to grasp how far the images complement

---

[55] Durkheim points out how far the gods have as much need of men as men do of gods, cf Mopsik: *Les Rites qui font Dieu*, which also shows how Kabbalah has developed a theurgy (*Shem Tov*; the ritual practices cause an effusion of the celestial world into earthly world). Man is in certain respects "the creator of the creator."

[56] Agamben, *The Kingdom and the Glory*, 230.

[57] Agamben, *The Kingdom and the Glory*, 242.

[58] Consequently, Agamben returns to Schmitt, who links democracy and acclamation inextricably and locates the modern form of this acclamation in public opinion.

[59] Agamben, *The Kingdom and the Glory*, 286–287.

the ritual, or at least lead to interpreting it and understanding it, and above all to experiencing it, in another way. It is worth highlighting again—once more through the iconography—the things that could not be considered here due to a lack of space: how the degree combines a contemplative approach, that of the mandala that the lodge tracing board constructs but which releases and develops energy—in a form that is all the more strong here because the image is a dynamic one—with an approach that is active, operative, and focused on action, as illustrated by the movement of the different corps, which truly set out amidst the wind of the standards and the sound of cannon fire!

Transforming the temple into a real game of snakes and ladders, which offers an invitation to concretely experience the spiral and *mise en abyme* of meanings, the appropriation of iconographic issues by the contemporary Masons, as I hope to have demonstrated, opens new perspectives for understanding the degree of Sublime Prince of the Royal Secret and the Royal Secret itself.

# Bibliography

*A. Sources:*

Iconographic sources are presented in the text of the article and the captions, and they are included in the bibliography below; the sources of the rituals are the following:

- The ritual I use here is that of the manuscript of the BNF listed under Nouv. Acq. Frçs 10960 (series from the Cabinet des Manuscrits entitled Nouvelles Acquisitions Françaises, therefore not part of the Masonic collections). The title of the ritual, which can be dated

to between 1810 and 1825, is Knight of Saint Andrew, Faithful Guardian of the Sacred Treasure and Valiant Prince of the Royal Secret. It has sometimes been called "Morin," a name that has in fact nothing to do with Morin and that I will not use here.
- Ms Baylot BNF FM4. 15, (also known as Ms St Domingue), 1764.
- Francken, Rituel, 1783, Aréopage Sources. The standard translation is by G. Lamoine, éd. SNES, 2007; this is the version from which I have quoted.

*B. Works consulted in preparing this article:*

Agamben, Giorgio. *The Kingdom and the Glory* (Stanford, CA: Stanford University Press, 2011).

Carruthers, Mary. *Machina memorialis, méditation, rhétorique et fabrication des images au Moyen Âge.* Paris: Gallimard, 2002.

Champeaux, Gérard, and S. Sterckx. *Introduction au monde des symboles.* Paris: Zodiaque, 1980.

Suprême Conseil du GC du REAA-GODF. *Deux siècles de REAA en France, 1804–2004.* Paris: Suprême Conseil du GC du REAA-GODF, 2004.

Fellous, Sonia. *Histoire de la Bible de Moïse Arragel.* Somogy: Paris, 2001.

Feddersen, Klaus C. F. *Die Arbeitstafel in der Freimaurerei,* Bayreuth Quellenkundliche Arbeit 16, "Der Forschungsloge," *Quatuor Coronati* 808 (1987).

Foucault, Michel. *Sécurité, territoire, population, Leçons au Collège de France, 1977-1978.* Paris: Gallimard, 2004.

Fromaget, Michel. *Le Symbolisme des quatre vivants*. Paris: Ed. Du félin, 1992.

Godwin, Malcom. *Angels, an Endangered Species*. New York: Simon and Schuster, 1990.

Horne, Alex. *Le Temple de Salomon dans la tradition maçonnique*. Paris: Ed. Du Rocher, 1994.

Jardin, Dominique. "Le Vingt-et-unième grade du REAA: le Noachite ou Chevalier Prussien et le 'noachisme.'" *Sources, Travaux de l'Aréopage* 6 (2007): 29–102

———. "Représentations du Centre à travers quelques exemples de tableaux de loge maçonniques du XVIIIe siècle." *Politica Hermetica* 22 (2008): 53–83.

———. *Emprunts opératifs, religieux et ésotériques dans les rituels et l'iconographie des tableaux de loge des systèmes français à hauts grades au XVIIIe siècle: Contribution à l'étude de la construction de la tradition maçonnique* (four volumes, 734 pages and 300 pages iconographic plates, thesis, EPHE and Université de Nice, Nice 2008).

———. *Voyages dans les tableaux de loge*. Paris: J-C Godefroy, 2011.

Kirk MacNulty, William. *La Franc-Maçonnerie, symboles, secrets et significations*. Paris: Seuil, 2006.

Lazar, Ion, "The Symbolic Camp of the 32: Mysteries of Sacred Geometry & Masonic Astronomy." *Hérédom* 18 (2010): 259–297

Lévy, Jean-Bernard. *Quelques moments de l'histoire du REAA*. Paris: La Hutte, 2012.

Lerbet, Georges. "La parole est dans le vent."

In *L'Ecossais* n°9, Suprème Conseil du GC du REAA-GODF, 2005, 60 and after.

Mopsik, Charles. *Les Grands textes de la cabale: les rites qui font Dieu*. Paris: Verdier, 2002.

Pasquier, Gilles, "Présentation et Traduction des manuscrits Graham' (1726)." In *La franc-maçonnerie, documents fondateurs*. Paris: L'Herne, 1991.

Pastoureau, Michel. *Traité d'héraldique*. 3rd edition. Paris: Picard, 1997.

Porset, Charles. *Les Philalèthes et les Convents de Paris. Une politique de la folie*. Paris: Champion, 1996.

———. "La vérité est une fable ou les philatèthes et la question du symbole." In *Symboles, Signes, langages sacrés pour une sémiologie de la franc-maçonnerie*, edited by Gian Mario Cazzaniga. Pisa: ETS, 1995.

The supplement of *Ordo ab Chao* 42 (2000), dedicated to the camp of the thirty-second degree and its tracing board, was not consulted.

# Freemasonry at the Inception of the Legion of Honor

Pierre Mollier[A]

In one of a number of conversations in which Lacépède reported his thoughts as Grand Chancellor of the Legion of Honor, Napoleon spoke to him of "the Temple I have ordered to be built," and asked him to move the work along.[1] Given that the worthiness and multiple Masonic responsibilities of the learned naturalist were well known in the literary circles of Paris, it is hard not to see in this a nod and a wink from the Emperor, whether he was an initiate or not.[2] In this way, from behind the mask of authority, Napoleon called on the personal values of his faithful follower; there was indeed work to be done to establish the new Order. The hypotheses that claim a Masonic influence on the creation of the Legion of Honor, and the choice of star that features in it, have been advanced numerous times, and research has been conducted to look into these matters.[3] I restrict myself here to a study of the possible links between the lodges and those who actually established, in practice, the administration of the award between 1802 and 1815. Its two main organizers, General Mathieu Dumas and Lacépède, were well-known masons, as indeed were some of the cohort leaders, and Cambacérès. But behind these great figures, might brothers of more modest rank also have contributed to the establishment of the Legion of Honor? Let us immerse ourselves in the daily activity of the Grand Chancellery under the Empire... and attempt to gain a better understanding of the milieu from which it recruited its craftsmen. This investigation into the men present in the early days of the Legion of Honor is also intended as a contribution to the study of the symbolism of power in France. This most eminent of our Orders played an undeniable role in the social representation of public authority, and of the elites, throughout the nineteenth century. To take an interest in the origins of the Legion of Honor is therefore also to study an aspect of the system of values upon which the construction of a new State in modern France took place.

---

[A] Director of the Grand Orient de France Library and of the Museum of Freemasonry (Paris).

[1] *Correspondance de Napoléon I*er *publiée par ordre de l'Empereur Napoléon III* (Paris: Henri Plon/J. Dumaine, 1863, T. 14, p. 64; "Letter 11437 – To M. Lacépède, Posen, December 11 1806. When you have presided over the first celebration to be held in the Temple I have ordered to be built, you may withdraw, but not before that time. I do not remember the decree to which you refer me in your letter. But what you may be sure of is my desire to make the grandest gesture in favor of the Legion, and to send to you in particular, proof of the high esteem in which I hold you. Napoleon."

[2] Napoleon is probably first referring to the construction of the Madeleine, for which the original intention was that it should be a temple in the ancient style to the glory of the nation, but the formulation is also striking in its Masonic tone. See Général P. Codechèvre, "Le comte de Lacépède premier Grand Chancelier de la Légion d'honneur," *Souvenir Napoléonien*, 268 (March 1973): 7-12.

[3] See Laurence Wodey, *L'insigne de la Légion d'honneur* (Paris: Cahiers du Musée de la Légion d'honneur et des Ordres de chevalerie, 2005).

# I - Lacépède among his Brothers

Officially named Grand Chancellor at the first session of the Grand Council on August 14 1803, Lacépède first had to confront the need to set up an administrative system for the Legion of Honor. In response to citizen Caédès, who offered him his services, he explained how such an administration was:

"indispensable in order to make it possible to execute the decrees of the Grand Council of the Legion of Honor. As soon as I was, to my great astonishment, named Grand Chancellor, I was faced with numerous small tasks. I made haste to appeal to those around me in order to arrange the small number of bureaus that I needed, old friends accustomed to my way of working, and persons chosen and employed in the commencement of the Legion for more than a year by Councilor of State Dumas, whom the general had, so to speak, handed on to me."[4]

Who were these "old friends accustomed to [his] way of working,"[5] of whose eminent role in establishing the administration of the Legion of Honor Lacépède informs us? The high proportion of Masonic relationships within the first "bureaus" of the new national Order suggests we should look to the lodges as the Grand Chancellor's recruiting ground.

As was the case with many of the officials of the Empire, Lacépède's membership of the masons was known. But it is important to remember that being a mason can mean different things in many very different situations. While for some, initiation and attendance at the lodge were undoubtedly a part of their philosophical training and an important aspect of their social life, for others, it may only have been a more circumstantial affiliation, more occasional and of no real significance. In order to attempt an assessment of the possible influence of the person he is studying, the historian must therefore first attempt to understand that person's level and degree of Masonic commitment.

The file on *Lacépède* is particularly full in this regard. He was initiated around 1776 in the Lodge La Sincérité in his native town Agen when he was 20 years old. In 1778-1779–at the age of 22–during his first visit to the capital, he was an active mason. We find him first on the register–that is, the list of members' names–of the *Frères Initiés* [Brothers Initiate] Lodge: "Bernard Germain, Étienne/de la Ville Comte de Lacépède/Colonel of Infantry/Member/ [born in] Agen [in] 1757/[staying at] Rue

---

[4] Letter from M. Lacépède to M. Caédès, 19 Fructidor, Year XI (September 6 1803). Archives of the Grande Chancellerie, Box marked "Grands Chanceliers 1803-1981," LHM D[1B], Dossier 3, Lacépède papers.

[5] In his *Autobiographie*, written in 1816, thus nearly 13 years later, Lacépède uses a similar expression again: "seconded by old friends whom I had gathered around me in order to form the grand Chancellery." This exciting document will be cited on several further occasions in this paper. It was published by Roger Hahn in the seventh edition of the magazine *Dix-huitième siècle* [*Eighteenth century*] (1975) under the title "L'autobiographie de Lacépède retrouvée [The autobiography of Lacépède found]," on pages 49-85. This text is firstly an explanation of the measures he took to defend his position in the first months of the Bourbon Restoration. It is therefore not reliable in respect of his real positions in the Revolution and under the Empire. Nevertheless, through its style and a number of anecdotes, it is quite informative about Lacépède the man, and his inclinations.

St. André des arts, hotel Château vieux."[6] The lodge at work seems to have brought together representatives of the wealthy bourgeoisie, counting among its members many merchants, and two bankers who were also dignitaries of the Grand Orient: Tassin and Valette. Perhaps Lacépède joined this lodge through Brother Cébet, who was also from Agen, and who was one of its most active members, spending a long time in the role of secretary. But the young Lacépède did not stay in Paris long, and a few months later he was recorded under the rubric "FF members of the *L∴ absent.*" with the comment "in Agen."[7] He does not appear in the lodge's registers again after 1780.

However, possibly from 1778,[8] but certainly from 1783, we find him as a member of one of the most prestigious lodges of the eighteenth century,[9] appearing on the register of the *Neuf Sœurs* [Nine Sisters] Lodge: "Ct de Lacépède, Colonel of the troops of the Empire, member of several academies, M∴*[aster]*, Absent." Listed at number 65, he takes his place between "Claude Joseph Vernet, of the Royal Academy of Painting" (No. 64) and "Jean-Antoine Houdon, of the Royal Academy of Painting" (No. 66).[10] In his autobiography, written at the beginning of the Bourbon Restoration, and from which any trace of Masonic allusions was carefully erased, he writes of his meetings with Franklin and Voltaire as being among the high points of his life. This lodge, and in particular its president, Benjamin Franklin, played an important role in Voltaire's last journey to Paris. Lacépède probably continued as an active mason in this illustrious company until the Revolution, but the details of his Masonic life during the period are unknown,[11] the archives of the *Neuf Sœurs* having disappeared. At any event, he was attached to the lodge, since he was one of those who crafted its return at the beginning of the nineteenth century.

In the 1780s, he certainly visited the famous lodge of the liberal aristocracy associated with Orléans, *La Candeur* [Innocence]. It counted among its members a childhood friend to whom he always remained close, Cyrus de Valence, a fellow Agenais: "In his earliest years [... he] made friends with the young Comte de Valence, and their friendship became so close that throughout their whole lives, they never stopped calling each other "brother" and exchanging tokens of their true brotherhood."[12]

---

[6] Register of the lodge of *Les Frères Initiés* [Brothers Initiate], register No. 3713, June 7 1779, archived June 23 1779, BnF, FM² 78 bis, f 123.

[7] Register of the lodge taken January 9 1779, idem, f [f] 122. His name is also found on the register published in 1784 by the *La Sincérité* Lodge in Agen in the office of Deputy Master.

[8] Register of the Brothers of the *Neuf Sœurs* Lodge [...] 5778, published as an appendix in Louis Amiable, *Une Loge Maçonnique d'avant 1789 – la Respectable Loge "les Neufs Sœurs."* (Paris: F. Alcan, 1897). Critical re-edition by Charles Porset (Paris: Edimaf, 1989) 392. The original document has disappeared.

[9] Louis Amiable, *Une Loge Maçonnique*, provides a history of this rather extraordinary lodge.

[10] The archives of the *Neuf Sœurs* Lodge disappeared in the nineteenth century. This list dated 1783 is a nineteenth-century copy preserved in the archives of the *La Clémente Amitié* [Merciful Friendship] Lodge, BnF, FM² 90, f°28v°.

[11] Amalric, however, emphasizes the friendship between him and Pastoret, one of the principal driving forces of the *Neuf Sœurs* at this time. "Notice historique sur la vie et les ouvrages de M. le Cᵗᵉ de Lacépède," extract from the *Revue Encyclopédique* (March 1826), Rignoux [printers], Paris.

[12] Amalric, "Notice historique," 4.

We do know that contrary to the version of events established by the radical-socialist brothers of the Third Republic, the Revolution, far from favoring Freemasonry, led to the closure of the lodges and the suspension of the Grand Orient. But beyond the cessation of activity for a period of time, the troubles of the Masons under the Terror encouraged them above all to proceed with great caution in their documentation when, after the revolutionary storm had passed, the lodges were revived. Why establish lists of members and archives that might turn out to be compromising were the situation once more to be overturned? Masonic activity picked up again in 1795 around some lodges. But it was only once the situation was stabilized with the Consulate, in 1800, that little by little, the Masonic bureaucracy would return to operation and the historian would have lists of members, compilations of minutes, and other files at his disposal once again. It was really only around 1803 that the Grand Orient re-established its administrative apparatus and its authority over the lodges.

This is the year when Lacépède, elected Junior Warden on September 30 1803, reappears among the papers of the Order. For the whole of the period of Empire he would, in the company of his friend Valence, be one of the *Grands Officiers* of the *Grand Orient de France*, Grand Administrator from 1804 until 1813, at which time he became Grand Treasurer. His lodge commitments include becoming the "Vénérable" [Worshipful Master] of the Saint-Napoléon Lodge in 1805, and he participated in the return to operation of the *Neuf Sœurs* in 1806. He was, of course, an honorary member of the *La Sincérité* Lodge in Agen.[13] He would also become a member of the Supreme Council of the French Empire for the Ancient and Accepted Scottish Rite. Despite the gaps in the archives, they do contain plenty of evidence of his Masonic activity. In the large registers that house the meticulous minutes of several Chambers of the *Grand Orient de France*, he is often found in the company of Cambacérès, who was also an *Ancien Régime* mason. He was therefore in all probability an active member of the "personal" lodge that the Archchancellor created in 1806, with the explicit name of *La Grande Maîtrise* [The Grand Mastership]. But, in the absence of archival sources, this latter point remains conjecture.

## II - The Lodge of the *Grande Chancellerie* [Grand Chancellery]

Under Lacépède's Mastership, the administration of the Grand Chancellery was organized into five divisions.[14] The heads of the first (Amalric), second (Davaux), and fifth (Lavallée[15]) divisions were well-known masons, as was Barouillet, the second-in-charge of the

---

[13] In 1809, BnF, FM² 132.

[14] Archives of the *Grande Chancellerie*, Box marked *"Personnel"*, LHM D² 1. Besides the Treasury and the department in charge of the *Maisons d'éducation* [schools for the families of members], the five divisions that managed the affairs of the Legion of Honor were "Dépêches [Dispatches]," "Pétitions [Petitions]," "Correspondance [Correspondence]," "Domaines [Areas of Work]," and "Titres [Titles]." See the organizational diagram of the *Grande Chancellerie* under the Empire in Laurence Wodey, *Guide de Recherche en histoire de la Légion d'honneur Musée national de la légion d'honneur et des ordres de chevalerie* (Saint-Rémy-en-l'eau/Paris: Hayot, 2002), 42.

[15] Davaux and Lavallée are in the registers of *Les Commandeurs du Mont-Thabor* [Commanders of Mount Tabor] Lodge; see the folder of correspondence between the lodge and the Grand Orient, BnF, FM² 65bis.

third division. Raoul, the lawyer in charge of legal matters was also an active mason, as were two of the five members of the cabinet: Tardif and Aussignac. Furthermore, Amalric–"General Secretary of the Legion of Honor"[16]–and Raoul[17] were dignitaries of the Grand Orient, the former being one of the "Great Experts of the Grand General Chapter", and the latter fulfilling the role of "Expert" in the *Grande Loge d'Administration*." Amalric, Davaux and Barouillet were also among the first to be taken on at the Grand Chancellery, on August 19 1803,[18] followed shortly after by Joseph Lavallée on October 24 1803. It is therefore very tempting to see in these brothers the "old friends accustomed to my way of working" referred to in the Grand Chancellor's private remarks!

Lacépède thus knew Jean-Baptiste Davaux[19]–"his celebrated friend" according to his own expression[20]–and Lavallée from the 1780s, since which time they had been masons together. Davaux was also a member of *Neuf Sœurs*. Lavallée was a member of another Paris lodge, *La Vérité* [The Truth], but in parallel with this he was also "one of the hardest-working members of the *Musée*,"[21] which was a subsidiary of the *Neuf Sœurs* lodge.[22] The former abbot, Amalric, became a friend of Lacépède's in 1795.[23] And Jean-Martin Barouillet had been a mason since 1790, at which date he is found as a member of the *La Parfaite Unité des Cœurs* [The Perfect Unity of Hearts] Lodge.[24]

The Masons of the Grand Chancellery also met in certain lodges. Amalric and Peyre,[25] the Comptroller of Estates, joined the *Saint-Napoléon* Lodge,[26] presided over by Lacépède. We also find them alongside

---

[16] This is how he is introduced in the new statutes of the Grand Orient promulgated in December 1804. *Extrait du livre d'Architecture de la R∴L∴ écossaise de Saint-Napoléon. De la constitution générale de l'ordre*, 58.

[17] See the *Calendrier maçonnique à l'usage des loges de la correspondance du Grand Orient de France*.

[18] "État nominatif des employés de la Légion d'Honneur depuis la fondation de l'ordre [Record of names of employees of the Legion of Honor since the foundation of the order]," Archives of the Grande Chancellerie, Box marked « Personnel » LHM D2 1.

[19] See Alain Le Bihan, *Francs-maçons parisiens du Grand Orient de France (Fin du XVIIIᵉ siècle)* (Paris: Bibliothèque Nationale, 1966), 150. On Jean-Baptiste Davaux, see Robert Henri Tissot and Camille Bellissant, eds, *Le Concert des Amateurs à l'Hôtel de Soubise (1769-1781). Une institution musicale parisienne en marge de la Cour* (Grenoble: CNRS-MSH-Alpes, June 2004). See in particular the chapter "Jean-Baptiste Davaux: un amateur-compositeur." Those wishing to hear his music can listen to the CD *La prise de la Bastille*, recorded by Concerto Köln, and published by Capriccio digital, where they will discover the *Symphonie concertante en sol pour deux violons principaux, mêlée d'airs patriotiques* by Citizen Davaux (1794).

[20] Lacépède, *Autobiographie*, 78.

[21] Entry on "Lavallée" in Louis Gabriel Michaud, *Biographie universelle ancienne et moderne*, nouvelle édition, (Paris, 1855, Tome X), 176.

[22] See Amiable, *Une Loge Maçonnique d'avant 1789*, 187-204.

[23] In 1825, he wrote: "the tender friendship with which he has honored us for 30 years, which we reciprocated with grateful fondness." Amalric, *Une Loge Maçonnique d'avant 1789*, 3.

[24] See Le Bihan, *Francs-maçons parisiens*, 55.

[25] Antoine-Marie Peyre (1770-1843). He was to refurbish the Hôtel de Salm between 1804 and 1812; he was responsible for the restoration of the Château d'Ecouen when, in 1806, it became part of the Grand Chancellery estate.

[26] See the folder of correspondence between the *Saint-Napoléon* Lodge and the Grand Orient, BnF, FM² 108, particularly the register for 1808.

Davaux and Raoul in the revival of the *Neuf Sœurs* in 1806.[27] Royer *fils* and Lejeune were in *Isis*. With the help of the "employees" Anglade, Fageot, Fleury, Lenex, and Pissot, Barouillet and Davaux helped Joseph Lavallée to create the *Commandeurs du Mont-Thabor* Lodge, where a quarter of the founders worked at the Grand Chancellery. They were later joined by Lafitte, Tardif, Aussignac, Behier, and Duteil. The Worshipful Master of the lodge was Joseph Lavallée, but there was also an honorary Worshipful Master, who was, of course, none other than Lacépède.

To gain a better insight into the circle of people who made the Grand Chancellery work, let us lift the veil that covers the mysterious meetings of the Respectable Lodge, *Les Commandeurs du Mont-Thabor.*[28] It is March 15 1808; the brothers come to the Masonic hall in much the same way as to a meeting of a social circle. After the presentation and the debate, some of the remainder of the evening is devoted to dinner, singing, and music. The meeting is presided over by Brother Lavallée (head of the fifth division). Seated to his left is the speaker, Mangourit–briefly Commissioner in Foreign Relations under the revolutionary regime, and in 1808, Secretary General of the Académie Celtique [since 1813, the *Société des Antiquaires de France* (Society of Antiquaries of France)], to which we shall return–, and to his right, the Lodge secretary, Vatinelle, "an employee

of the Official Journal, *Le Moniteur,*" assisted by Marie, a close colleague of Lavallée at the Grand Chancellery. At the other end, "in the West," the Senior Warden is Bazaine, an officer in *Ponts et Chaussées* [Corps of Bridges and Roads] and a tutor at the École Polytechnique, and the Junior Warden, Rey, a *général de division* [Major General]. The music used to alleviate the austere nature of Masonic work is in the hands of Davaux (head of the second division). In various offices, and "holding the columns," we find no fewer than eleven other brothers who work at the Grand Chancellery. It comes as no surprise that one of the acclamations of the lodge was "*Honneur et Patrie*"[29]–the motto of the Legion of Honor. That evening, the agenda included the ceremony awarding a patent that allowed the lodge to work in the "Scottish Philosophic Rite," an important document personally signed by His Supreme Highness Brother Prince Archchancellor, and delivered to them by Brother General Rouyer,[30] who was also treasurer of the ninth cohort of the Legion, alongside his leader, Brother Marshal Lannes, grand administrator of the *Grand Orient de France.*

The lodge meets fortnightly. Some months later, on September 6 1808, Joseph Lavallée is ill, and so the brothers gather under the watchful chairmanship of their "Honorable Worshipful Master, arrayed as the priest of the natural sciences and of the National Honors Committee"[31] [sic], the

---

[27] *Annuaire de 5838 de la L∴ des Neuf-sœurs… des tableaux des membres composant la L∴ en 1783 et 1806* (Paris: Dondey-Dupré, 1838), 61-64.

[28] SThe report on the principal works of 1808 was published in a pamphlet, *Commandeurs du Temple du Mont Thabor, Rit Ecossais Philosophique, à l'O[rient] de Paris* (Paris, Porthmann, 5809 [1809]), 110.

[29] *Commandeurs*, 41-42.

[30] Jean-Pascal Rouyer (Pézenas 1761- Bruxelles 1819). On his political and military career, see Georges Six, *Dictionnaire biographique des généraux et amiraux français de la Révolution et de l'Empire* (Paris: Saffroy, 1934, Tome II), 401.

[31] *Commandeurs*, 44.

Most Illustrious Brother de Lacépède. The joint speaker, the lawyer Brother Roger, delivers a talk on the symbolism of the solstices and equinoxes in relation to the Feast of Saint John. It is suffused with the theories of Dupuis[32] regarding religions in the great civilizations as interpretations of the revolutions of the sun, and with the doctrines of the *Idéologues*.

On December 17 1808, Brother Mangourit offers a panorama of the history of Freemasonry. Well in tune with the ideas of the time, he presents it as the heir to a long line of initiates stretching from the mystery cults of Antiquity to the Templars. Links to the Order of the Temple can be found in the Scottish Philosophic Rite professed by the lodge. One of its most eminent degrees is that of *Chevalier de l'Aigle Blanc et Noir* [Commander of the White and Black Eagle], or Kadosh, said to be a continuation of the august ceremonies of the medieval Order. In it, the member elect is given an explanation of the masons as descendants of the Templars unjustly persecuted in the fourteenth century, some of whom found refuge in Scotland in the lodges of stoneworkers. Masonry is indeed one of the places in which an interest in the Middle Ages and chivalric imagery reappeared in the 1740s, and developed throughout the second half of the eighteenth century.[33] Auguste Viatte suggested it

should be seen as one of the "hidden sources of Romanticism."[34] In such a circle, Joseph Lavallée and his friends happily favor each other with the modest title of "Noble Commander"!

The "Lodge of the Grand Chancellery"–as we should indeed call it–therefore combined the philosophy of Voltaire with chivalric rites, a mixture that may appear odd to us today, but which was typical of Masonic circles of the time.[35] The lodge was particularly proud of the correspondence it maintained with other lodges, and of receiving visits such as that from the "Most Illustrious Brother Baron Girard, Brigadier General, and Worshipful Master [of the Lodge] *Les Frères de la Grande Armée* [The Brothers of the Great Army],"[36] or one a few weeks later from General Lassalle. But behind the cumbersome rhetoric, we can also discern comments that are not completely without political implications. Thus, in one digression the speaker, Mangourit, recalls how important it is "for those who hold public authority not to compromise their reputations by the way they wield it." Homage is of course rendered to Brother Grand Chancellor, but in very interesting terms at a time when Napoleon was creating the nobility of the Empire: "This gentle name of 'brother'"– the illustrious Lacépède is informed–"becomes ever more precious in our engaging

---

[32] Dupuis, French Citizen, *Origine de tous les Cultes ou Religion Universelle* (Paris: H. Agasse, Year III of the one and indivisible Republic [1794-95]). See Claude Rétat, "Lumière et ténèbres du Citoyen Dupuis." *Chroniques d'Histoire Maçonnique*, 1999 50: 5-68.

[33] See Pierre Mollier, "Les rituels de la Maçonnerie Templière, un cycle légendaire au siècle des Lumières. Paper presented at the symposium *Le légendaire maçonnique: rêve et initiation*, *"Renaissance Traditionnelle*, 129: 29-40.

[34] Auguste Viatte, "Les sources occultes du romantisme, Illuminisme, théosophie, 1770-1820" (PhD diss., University of Paris: H. Champion, 1928).

[35] See François Cavaignac, "Légende templière et imaginaire maçonnique dans le théâtre profane en France au XIXᵉ siècle." In *Deux siècles de Rite Ecossais Ancien Accepté en France* (Paris: Dervy, 2004), 143-161.

[36] *Commandeurs*, 76.

meetings, in view of the fact that the public good, and personal interests within society, require honors which reflect a commingling of the two. It assumes for us a new charm, in that you are obliged to receive, as we are to give to you, these titles, which do not detach you from the reasoned equality we so pleasantly find here; and you will find true joy at our fraternal meetings in your abandonment of your exalted rank, and in your consent to being no more than a man; so we say to you that you lose nothing by it; but when you are among a society of free men, you will sense how much you gain by it."[37]

## III - *Joseph Lavallée and the Ideology of the Early Legion of Honor*

Although there were many masons among the officials who set up the Legion of Honor, only one of them–a very close colleague of the Grand Chancellor–was entrusted with the essential task of writing the first book on the new Order.[38] Knowing, as we do, the level of attention given by the Napoleonic regime to the power of symbols, it is unlikely that the publication by Joseph Lavallée, in 1807, of the *Annales nécrologiques de le Légion d'Honneur*[39] [Annals of the deceased members of the Legion of Honor] came about simply as a matter of personal initiative. Furthermore, this publication does seem to be a direct continuation of his work at the head of the fifth division, the "Titles" department. Lacépède–and beyond him, probably

the Emperor himself–certainly supported this book, and indeed even commanded it; the long subtitle of the work explains its content: "Notes on the lives, outstanding actions, military and administrative service, and scientific and literary works of the members of the Legion of Honor who have died since the creation of this institution, dedicated to H.M. the Emperor and King, Supreme Head of the Legion of Honor, and drawing upon authentic memoirs." Historians have asked themselves many questions regarding the true nature of Napoleon's creation: was the Legion of Honor a version of the old orders of the *Ancien Régime*, adapted to the tastes of the day, or was it a new kind of institution? It seems clear that Lavallée's book may have something to tell us about–dare we use the word!–the ideology of the early Legion of Honor.

In the preface, the line unambiguously taken by the author is that it is a continuation of the ideas of the Revolution: "The decoration promised by the establishment of the Legion of Honor is a prize that all men can fight for [...] what a noble idea to offer men the prospect of a distinction for which the indispensable prerequisite is the exercise of all the virtues [...] to force pride itself to become the agent of perfection."[40] The book aims to offer an "insight into the incalculable services already rendered by the Legion of Honor [... it is] for the generation now being born, the most useful guide to consult [...it offers] at last that hitherto unheard of thing: equality between Citizens, guaranteed even

---

[37] *Commandeurs*, 20.

[38] Previously, different annual reports had been published, including also the regulations and some of the discussions of the Order, but the Annales were the first attempt to offer a clear presentation of the Legion of Honor.

[39] Joseph Lavallée, *Annales nécrologiques de la Légion d'Honneur* (Paris: F. Buisson, 1807).

[40] Lavallée, *Annales nécrologiques*, x.

in the matter of distinctions."[41] While La-vallée does not miss an opportunity to pay emphatic homage on numerous occasions to the genius of the "Hero of the French," he also puts forward the idea that the *Annales de la Légion d'Honneur* will be the best refutation of those who would defame the "Great Nation and all the principles of probity, justice, and loyalty [...which are the] fruits of the French Revolution." The author clearly forges a link to weapons of honor, and strives to offer us a veritable literary "*Arc de Triomphe.*" "Our book, avenger of a Nation outraged, [will] redress these lies before the Nations of the world, [it will say] to future races: Here are the men whose mores, vigilance and deeds at that time, illuminated the Magistrature, the Administration, the Diplomacy, the Liberal Arts, the Industry, the Commerce, and the Priesthood of this vast Empire, read and pass judgment."[42] We find ourselves here in a tableau by David!

The personality of Joseph Lavallée may also shed light on the nature of the project. The head of the fifth division of the Grand Chancellery was far from being a mere bureaucrat. The title page of the book lists the titles he bore: "secretary in perpetuity of the *Société Philotechnique de Paris*, Member of the *Académie Celtique* and the *Société Académique des Enfants d'Apollon*, as well as the *Société Royale des sciences de Gottingue* and the *Académies* of Dijon, Nancy, and so on." Membership of the *Académie Celtique*, to which Lacépède also belonged, indicates an ideological profile. This Napo-leonic institution, created in 1805, has long been neglected by historians, who see it simply as an avatar of Celtomania. In fact, as the work of Jean-Yves Guiomar,[43] Mona Ozouf and Nicole Belmont[44] has been showing for some years, it was a wide circle of intellectuals who gathered under that colorful heading. This direct ancestor of the Société des *Antiquaires de France* really represents the beginnings of French ethnography–but its scholarly research was conducted in a particular ideological context. The Catholic *Ancien Régime* is, in a way, seen as a parenthesis, and it therefore comes as no surprise that Brother Lavallée's *Annales nécrologiques de la Légion d'honneur* should present its fallen members as ancient heroes.

The fact is that the author never denied his taste for the philosophical aspects and ideas of the Enlightenment. Born Marquis of Bois-Robert in 1747, he was an infantry captain in the Champagne regiment between 1770 and 1780, and divided his time between a fairly dilettante military life and the salons of Paris, where he endeavored to write poetry and novels. In 1789, the Revolution saw him released from the Bastille, where his family had had him locked up because of his unruly escapades! He "repudiated his hereditary nobility and enthusiastically adopted the new political principles." He published a *Discours d'un philosophe à la nation française, la veille de l'ouverture des États-généraux, ou le Ralliement des trois ordres...* [Discourse of a philosopher to the French nation on the eve of

---

[41] Lavallée, *Annales nécrologiques*, xi.

[42] Lavallée, *Annales nécrologiques*, xii.

[43] Jean-Yves Guiomar, "La Révolution Française et les origines celtiques de la France," *Annales Historiques de la Révolution Française* (1992/1): 64-84.

[44] Nicole Belmont, *Paroles païennes, mythe et folklore, des frères Grimm à P. Saintyves* (Paris: Imago, 1986), 180 p.; *Aux Sources de l'ethnologie française, l'Académie Celtique* (Paris: Editions du C.T.H.S., 1995), 478 p.

the opening of the Estates-General, or the Assembly of the three orders...], and in 1793, a *Fête des Sans-culottes, couplets chantés dans un banquet civique, le dimanche 6 janvier, l'an IIᵉ de la République française* [Festival of the *sans-culottes*, couplets sung at a civic banquet, January 6 Year II of the French Republic]. Michaud,[45] who evidently knew him well, paid homage to him on an intellectual level: "Lavallée combined a naturally very active mind with solid and varied instruction. He spoke most European languages, and had undertaken a thorough study of the theory of the Arts. This work being easy for him, he partook of the writing of many books."[46] But as an old royalist, Michaud could not help but disparage certain of those books "for their most excessive exaltation of republican principles." Lavallée was very representative of the "Late Enlightenment", modeled on the Ideologues, and attached to the principles of 1789, if not all of the excesses of the Revolution. After the failure of the Directory, their ideal regime, many of them were keen to make an accommodation with despotism, provided it was enlightened despotism and kept away from the clergy, the Bourbons, and the émigrés.

The officials of the Grand Chancellery under the Empire were all friends bound together by twenty years of companionship through troubled times. Convinced of the ideas of the Enlightenment in their youth, experts and amateurs in arts and letters, they would put their talents and their culture at the service of the new Order, that Legion which was based on virtue instead of on birth, as in the dark days of the *Ancien Régime*. They had read in Montesquieu that an enlightened regime could only be established if built by virtuous men; it was the purpose of the Legion of Honor to bring such men together. The project was imbued with the great significance of what was at stake, and with a nobility of ambition. When the "legitimate sovereign" returned, Lacépède fell into disgrace, Davaux was retired, and as for the aforementioned Marquis of Bois-Robert, the ex-*sans-culottes* Lavallée, he went into exile in London, where he died in 1816.

It would, nevertheless, be at variance with reality to see the Legion of Honor as "a product of freemasonry" in the caricatured sense of the term, or to overstate the role of widespread Masonic membership in the workings of the Grand Chancellery. For example, life in the lodge was only one part of what linked Lacépède and Davaux. They were also both musicians, like Lavallée and Barouillet, and met at the (musical) *Société Académique des Enfants d'Apollon*. "From 1800 to 1810, Davaux had offered brilliant concerts at his house, where skillful players could be heard."[47] Freemasonry,[48] learned

---

[45] Michaud's biographical notes on Davaux and Lavallée are particularly interesting inasmuch as their assessments indicate a personal knowledge of the two men.

[46] Michaud, *Biographie universelle*.

[47] Michaud, *Biographie universelle*.

[48] We should not exaggerate the role of Masonic links, but it is nonetheless remarkable to note the importance it may have had for someone like Davaux, for example, in his "non-Masonic" existence after the Revolution. Before 1789, he was secretary to the Prince of Guémenée. "Events" of course led to him losing his employment. During the time of the Directory, he was protected by Beumonville, who arranged for him to enter the Ministry of War. Under the Empire, it was Lacépède who called him to his side. Under the Restoration, when his post was eliminated, he owed the attribution of a small pension to the intervention of MacDonald.

societies, and musical societies are simply the different forms of relationship enjoyed by Lacépède with his various friends, who are indeed an important part of his life. Lacépède was a faithful friend. His autobiography gives a striking insight into this character trait. His life is shaped by a succession of meetings with friends, and his writing is full of expressions like "my dear friend," "my admirable friend," "my celebrated friend," "my esteemed friend," "my illustrious friend"... Moreover, those administrators of the Grand Chancellery who appear not to be masons do appear to have a particular relationship with him, like the head of the secretariat, de Bock, who is his "kinsman,"[49] or the Jubés, who belonged to his wife's family. Amalric highlights the extent to which Lacépède included an affective side in his professional relationships, "[treating] those he had chosen to work with him like a father."[50]

While the Legion of Honor is not the work of the masons, the strong presence of "brothers" in its early years is an element–among others–that contributed toward forging its identity. Their imprint extended beyond 1815, in fact, as some of the "bureaus" remained in place,[51] and the new Grand Chancellor, MacDonald, was also an old mason.[52] What values did these men transmit to France's foremost national Order? In the eighteenth century, freemasonry acted as a bridge between two worlds. In its rites and symbolism, it held to the traditional institutions of the old France, with brotherhoods, craft guilds, and orders of chivalry. In its social dimension, with the debates and channels of exchange that it created, it is firmly bound up with the Enlightenment, of which it became a vector. This dual nature undoubtedly affected Lacépède and "his friends." It was this dual inheritance that they placed in the cradle of the new Legion of Honor, and that is still today a major part of its identity: "I wanted this wonderful institution," wrote the Grand Chancellor, "to help provide the unshakeable foundations of public morality, to re-establish the cultivation of true honor, and to bring the French chivalry of the past back to life under new emblems, purified of the excessive effects of centuries of ignorance, and embellished by what it might take from the centuries of Enlightenment."[53]

---

[49] *Lacépède, Autobiographie,* 74.

[50] Amalric, "Notice historique,"12.

[51] Among the important "historic" officials, Amalric, with his less militant past and calmer temperament, remained in place.

[52] A member of the *Le Centre des Amis* [The Friends' Center] Lodge, where he was probably received in 1795, grand administrator of the Grand Orient under the Empire, he would become its second and then its first Assistant Grand Master under the Restoration.

[53] Lacépède, *Autobiographie,* 74-75.

*Ritual, Secrecy, and Civil Society - Volume 2 - Number 2 - Winter 2014*

# The "Secret Life" of Sylvestre de Sacy (Orientalism in Freemasonry I)

Thierry Zarcone[A]

*This study, dedicated to Jean-Louis Bacqué-Grammont, allows me to pay homage to the man who, during his time as director of the Institut Français d'Etudes Anatoliennes (French Institute of Anatolian Studies) in Istanbul almost 25 years ago, welcomed us to Turkey and served as our guide, and then passed on the rudiments of the Ottoman language and the historian's profession.*

Abbreviations and English meanings:

- **Planche Travaux MLE 1805** (Scottish Mother Lodge Board of Works 1805): *Planche des travaux de la R∴[espectable] M∴[ère] L∴[oge] Ecossaise de Saint-Alexandre d'Ecosse à l'O∴ [rient] de Paris, tracée à l'occasion de la Fête de la Saint-Jean d'été, le 21e j. du 4e m∴[ois] 5805* (Paris: F∴[rère] Porthman, 1805).

- **Tableau des Frères MLE 1809** (Scottish Mother Lodge Table of Brothers 1809): *Tableau des F∴[rères] composant la R∴[espectable] M∴[ère] L∴[oge] Ec∴[ossaise] de France à l'O∴ [rient] de Paris, Précédé du verbal de la réception dans l'ordre, du F∴[rère] Askeri-Khan, Oncle de l'Empereur régnant en Perse, son Ambassadeur près la Cour de France* (Paris: F∴[rère] Porthmann Imprimeur, 1809).

- **Annales Maç. MLE 1807, 1809, 1810** (Scottish Mother Lodge Masonic Annals 1807, 1809, 1810): *Annales maç. Dédiées à son altesse sérénissime le prince Cambacérès – séance solennelle pour la réception dans l'ordre des F.-M. du F. Askeri-Khan, ambassadeur de Perse près la Cour de France, extraits des registres d'architecture de la R.M.L. Ec. de France à l'O . de paris*, (Paris: Caillot, 1807-1810, 8 vols.).

- **Annuaire Maç. MLE 1810** (Scottish Mother Lodge Masonic Yearbook 1810): *Annuaire maç∴[onniques] A l'usage des LL∴[oges] Et chap∴[itres] agrégés à la R∴[espectable] M∴[ère] L∴[oge] E∴[cossaise] du rite philosophique en France* (Paris: F∴[rère] Porthmann, Imprimeur, 1810).

- **Annuaire Maç. MLE 1811** (Scottish Mother Lodge Masonic Yearbook 1811): *Annuaire maçonnique A l'usage des LL∴[oges] Et chap∴[itres] agrégés à la R∴[espectable] M∴[ère] L∴[oge] E∴[cossaise] du rite philosophique en France, siégeante à l'Or∴[ient] de Paris* (Paris: F∴[rère] Porthmann, Imprimeur, 1811).

- **Annuaire Maç. MLE 1812** (Scottish Mother Lodge Masonic Yearbook 1812): *Annuaire maçonnique A l'usage des LL∴[oges] Et chap∴[itres] agrégés à la R∴[espectable] M∴[ère] L∴[oge] E∴[cossaise] du rite philosophique en France, siégeante à l'Or∴[ient] de Paris* (Paris: F∴[rère] Porthmann, Imprimeur, 1812).

- **Annuaire Maç. MLE 1813** (Scottish Mother Lodge Masonic Yearbook 1813): *Annuaire maçonnique A l'usage des LL∴[oges] Et chap∴[itres] agrégés à la R∴[espectable] M∴[ère] L∴[oge] E∴[cossaise] du rite philosophique en France, siégeante à l'Or∴[ient] de Paris* (Paris: F∴[rère] Porthmann, Imprimeur, 1813).

- **Annuaire Maç. MLE 1818** (Scottish Mother Lodge Masonic Yearbook 1818): *Annuaire maçonnique A l'usage des LL∴[oges] Et chap∴[itres] agrégés à la R∴[espectable] M∴[ère] L∴[oge] E∴[cossaise] de France de St.-Alexandre d'Ecosse et le Contrat Social réunis à l'Or∴[ient] de Paris* (Paris: F∴[rère] Porthmann, Imprimeur, 1818).

---

[A] University of Aalborg

The son of a notary, Antoine Isaac Silvestre de Sacy (1758–1838) is the emblematic figure of French and perhaps even European Orientalism. After studying several Semitic languages—Hebrew, Syriac, and Arabic, as well as Persian—Sacy made a name for himself thanks to his work in translation. The young scholar was not even thirty when, in 1785, the king made him one of the eight free associates attached to the Académie des Inscriptions (Academy of Inscriptions) By then, Sacy had been appointed councillor, in 1781, at the Cour des Monnaies (Paris Court of Currencies). In 1791, Louis XVI promoted him to chief commissioner of this court, but he abandoned this role in 1792, when the king fled at the time of the rise of the Republic. To escape the troubles in France at the time, the scholar retired for four years with his wife to a village in Brie, where he spent his time studying and gardening.[1] In 1793, he published his *Mémoires sur les antiquités de la Perse* (*Memoirs on the Antiquities of Persia*), and he then became chair in Arabic at the new Ecole spéciale des langues orientales vivantes (Special Academy for Modern Oriental Languages) created by the Convention in 1795.[2] He taught there for over forty years, until his death in 1838. This establishment for the training of interpreters and diplomats expected its professors not only to teach, but also to write a grammar of the language in which they specialized. Sacy was no exception to the rule, and in 1810, he published a grammar of Arabic, which was praised for its quality

by the academic world.[3] Over the following years, he gained many honors and teaching posts in prestigious establishments. In 1806, Sacy was appointed professor of Persian at the Collège de France, and Napoleon made him a baron in 1814. One year later, Sacy nevertheless gladly welcomed the return of the Bourbons, having never hidden Legitimist views on the matter. That same year, he became rector at the University of Paris. In 1833, he worked as inspector of oriental types at the Imprimerie royale (Royal Printworks), curator of oriental manuscripts at the Bibliothèque royale (Royal Library), and then permanent secretary of the Académie des Inscriptions et Belles-Lettres (Academy of Inscriptions and Literature). Moreover, in 1822, he was one of the founders of the Société asiatique (Asian society), where the Orientalist science would flourish, and he was its first president until 1825. Today, there are busts of him in several important locations for science and learning in Paris: the Ecole des langues orientales, the Institut de France, and the Collège de France.

Alongside such roles, the scholar was invited to participate in the political life of the country. He was deputy for the Seine in 1808, and was admitted to the Chamber of Peers in 1832. In 1828, he published an anonymous work exposing his political views, signed "a former member of the Chamber of Deputies." In it, Sacy complained that French society had not changed (undoubtedly since the Revolution) and that it still had "the same disregard for legitimate

---

[1] Toussaint Reinaud, *Notice historique et littéraire sur M. le Baron Silvestre de Sacy, lue à la séance générale de la Société asiatique le 25 juin 1838*, 2nd ed. (Paris: Librairie orientale de Ve Doncey-Dupré, 1838), 19.

[2] Hartwig Derenbourg, "Esquisse biographique," in *Silvestre de Sacy (1758–1838)*, ed. Georges Salmom (Cairo: Imprimerie de l'Institut français d'archéologie orientale, 1905), xv.

[3] Derenbourg, "Esquisse biographique," xviii.

authority" and the "same barely concealed hatred for religion." Looking back at the Empire, he writes that:

> We are far from regretting the tyranny that we have only ever served by protesting against its abuses, and because victory that was faithful to its flags ennobled our serfdom. However, because it has fallen, and with its fall a system of government that better conforms to the natural rights of man has been proclaimed, like a pact between he who gives orders and those who obey, our duty is to ensure that civil liberties are maintained.

Finally, Sacy confesses that he is "a Christian, a citizen, a royalist, and nothing more."[4] It is clear that the man of the Ancien Régime had moved into the new century, although without renouncing his views. Very quickly, scholars in Europe paid homage to this exceptional Orientalist, who was elected by the learned societies and academies of several countries. His 1838 obituary in the Bulletins de l'Académie royale des sciences et belles-lettres de Bruxelles describes him as "the elder, and in many ways, the master of Europe's Orientalists."[5] As well as teaching the Arabic and Persian languages, Sacy constantly engaged in passionate and devoted study of Muslim religion and culture. He was a very productive researcher: from 1783 to 1838, he published over four hundred texts, books, articles, and translations of Arabic and Persian texts, on a wide variety of subjects: epigraphy, numismatics, the history of Arabic dynasties and religion, and Arabic and Persian poetry.[6] Although Sacy taught modern Oriental languages to many interpreters and diplomats at the Ecole spéciale, he also trained generations of young French and European scholars and laid the foundations for the new Orientalist science.[7]

I will not expand further on the life of this brilliant Orientalist, since there are already many high-quality works and articles on this subject.[8] However, this rich and full career conceals a hidden side, a "secret life" never examined by biographers, from the *Notice littéraire* (*Literary Notice*) written by his student and friend Joseph Toussaint Reinaud (who was also his successor as chair of Arabic at the Ecole spéciale des langues orientales), to François Pouillon's *Dictionnaire des orientalistes de langue française* (*Dictionary of French-Language Orientalists*).[9] In fact, the father of French Orientalism chose to be initiated into the mysteries of Freema-

---

[4] Un ancien membre de la Chambre des députés, *Où allons-nous et que voulons-nous? ou la vérité à tous les partis* (Paris: chez Petit, libraire, 1827), 1, 7, 12.

[5] *Bulletins de l'Académie Royale des Sciences et Belles-Lettres de Bruxelles* 5 (1838): 137–138.

[6] See the list of his publications in Derenbourg, "Esquisse biographique," lxi–cxiv.

[7] Derenbourg, "Esquisse biographique," liv–lviii. On Sacy and Orientalism, see Christian Décobert, "L'Orientalisme des Lumières à la Révolution, selon Sylvestre de Sacy," *Revue du Monde Musulman et de la Méditerranée. Les Arabes, les Turcs et la Révolution Française* 52–53 (1989): 49–62.

[8] See also the proceedings of the 2001 conference dedicated to him: "Silvestre de Sacy (1758–1838): le projet européen d'une science orientaliste" (Institut du monde arabe and Ecole normale supérieur, Paris, 2001).

[9] Reinaud, *Notice historique et littéraire sur M. le Baron Silvestre de Sacy*; Sylvette Larzul, "Sylvestre de Sacy," in Dictionnaire des orientalistes de langue française, ed. François Pouillon (Paris: IISMM—Karthala, 2008), 897–898.

sonry, and belonged to this society for over thirty years. This fact remained a secret until the present day, and therefore never made it out of lodge archives. It is difficult to understand exactly who Silvestre de Sacy the Freemason was due to his ambiguous Masonic career, which mirrored Christian Décobert's description of his personality.[10]

## An Enigmatic Masonic Career

We know almost nothing of the Masonic life of Sylvestre de Sacy, who was initiated shortly before or after turning thirty, and before the Revolution, into a Parisian Lodge of unknown name. At the time, the young scholar was a councillor at the Cour des Monnaies. The Revolution, and in particular the Terror, caused almost all lodges to close. They only reopened under the Consulate, from 1800. We do not know whether Sacy reentered the lodges at this point, because his name does not reappear until 1809 in the members list of the Mère Loge Ecossaise de France (Scottish Mother Lodge of France), one of the main French Masonic obediences, which had numerous members from the country's political, financial, and intellectual elite. The lawyer Claude-Antoine Thory, who was one

of the dignitaries and for a long time the president of this obedience, and who was active from 1801 to 1821 or 1822, addressed his members in 1805, stating that:

> you have affiliated or given the light to a multitude of *Artists, Scholars, Servicemen, distinguished Merchants, skilled Doctors, enlightened Jurisconsults*, all of whom, by bringing the knowledge of their age here, have added to the collection of lights that shine in all parts of this ancient workshop.[11]

Sylvestre de Sacy is presented as follows in the yearbooks of the Mother Lodge: "SILVESTRE de Sacy, member of the Institute" (1809) and "SILVESTRE de Sacy (the Knight), member of the Institute" (1812).[12] He also appears in the yearbooks of the same obedience for 1810, 1813, and 1818.[13] Moreover, his name features in the list of "honorary members of the R∴ [espectable] M∴ [other] L∴ [odge], after twenty-one years of service," a list that in 1809 contained sixteen brothers. In 1818, Sacy, still considered an honorary member of the obedience, was joined by his fellow academic Aubin-Louis Millin (1759–1818), an archaeologist and curator of medals at the Bibliothèque nationale.[14] It seems

---

[10] Décobert, "L'Orientalisme des Lumières à la Révolution," 50.

[11] Planche Travaux MLE 1805 (Scottish Mother Lodge Board of Works 1805): 10. On the history of this obedience, see Pierre Chevallier, *Histoire de la franc-maçonnerie française* (Paris: Fayard, 1974) 2:54–70; Jacques Tuchendler, "Histoire abrégée de la R.L. Saint Alexandre d'Écosse de l'Ancien Régime à la Restauration," *Renaissance Traditionnelle* 138–140 (2004): 111–188.

[12] Tableau des Frères MLE 1809 (Scottish Mother Lodge Table of Brothers 1809), 83; Annuaire Maç. MLE 1812 (Scottish Mother Lodge Masonic Yearbook 1812), 88.

[13] Annuaire Maç. MLE 1810 (Scottish Mother Lodge Masonic Yearbook 1810), 120; Annuaire Maç. MLE 1813 (Scottish Mother Lodge Masonic Yearbook 1813), 75; Annuaire Maç. MLE 1818, 18.

[14] Annuaire Maç. MLE 1818 (Scottish Mother Lodge Masonic Yearbook 1818), 18. On Millin and Freemasonry, see Claude Rétat, "Revers de la science Aubin-Louis Millin, Alexandre Lenoir," in Rêver l'archéologie au XIXe siècle: de la science à l'imaginaire, ed. Eric Perrin-Saminalayar (St Etienne: Université de St Etienne, 2001), 97–119.

that Sacy was received as a Freemason in around 1788. However, an extract from the Mother Lodge ruling on honorary members suggests that the Parisian lodge that initiated Sacy was the Contrat Social Lodge. It states:

> Art. II. The Members of the ancient Contrat Social are, by rights, Members of the R∴ [espectable] Scottish Mother Lodge of France. They will belong to two distinct classes: the Honoraries after twenty-one years of service, and the active members.

Pierre Chevallier and Alain Le Bihan drew up a list of this lodge's members, from the time of its founding in 1776 until its works ended in 1792, but Sacy's name does not feature.[16] We can therefore suppose that he may have been initiated to the Contrat Social Lodge in the Revolutionary period, and that because of the political troubles, his name could not appear on the lodge register. However, we should not dismiss the possibility that Sacy may have been received into another Parisian lodge, only later joining the Mother Lodge. Only long and detailed research in the Masonic archives kept in the manuscripts section of France's Bibliothèque nationale might allow us to reconstruct the Orientalist's early Masonic career.[17]

Supposing that Sacy was received as a Freemason in 1788, and given that his name features in the yearbook of the Scottish Mother Lodge of France in 1818, we can infer that he remained faithful to the Masonic order for at least thirty years. The Mother Lodge, which has a rich library, holds one of the scholar's first works, and a library catalog extract readily states that the Orientalist is a brother. In fact, a "Notice on the general archives" of the *Annuaire pour l'année 5811* [1811] (5811 [1811] yearbook) mentions the "Memoirs on the Antiquities of Persia by 'Brother Sylvestre de Sacy.'"[18] The same yearbook indicates that the obedience's library is divided into seven sections, and that the last consists of:

> works entirely foreign to Freemasonry, including many writings on the Sciences, the Arts, Literature, History, Natural History, Medicine, Anatomy, and other works, some of which have been donated by the authors themselves, members of the Respectable Scottish Mother Lodge.

These books include "*the Histoire des inquisitions by Brother J. de Lavallée . . . The Rapports* by Brother *Lebreton*, Permanent Secretary of Fine Arts at the Institute," and finally, "Mémoires sur les antiquités de la Perse by Brother *Sylvestre de Sacy*."[19]

---

[15] Annuaire Maç. MLE 1810 (Scottish Mother Lodge Masonic Yearbook 1810), 34.

[16] Pierre Chevallier and Alain Le Bihan, *Histoire de Saint Jean d'Ecosse du Contrat Social Mère Loge Ecossaise de France* (Paris: Ivoire-Clair, 2002).

[17] Nor does his name feature in the listings of the Saint Jean d'Ecosse Lodge, which joined with the Contrat Social Lodge in 1806 to form the Mother Lodge (Paris: Bibliothèque nationale de France, Manuscripts section, Fonds Maçonnique/Masonic archives: shortened to BnF FM): FM² 100 bis.

[18] Reproduced in Claude Rétat, "Un temple à côté du temple. Le Muséum mystérieux de Thory," *Renaissance Traditionnelle*, 123–124 (2000): 244.

[19] Annuaire Maç. MLE 1811 (Scottish Mother Lodge Masonic Yearbook 1811), 100.

Although these clues provide evidence that Sylvestre de Sacy was a Freemason, they are far from clarifying the reasons for his alliance to the Masonic order, or his feelings about the changes to the institution after the Revolution. To my knowledge, Sacy never confessed to being a Freemason. Did he join the order under the Empire, for corporatist reasons, wishing to be part of the "imperial club" where the moneyed and intellectual elites gathered, often including several members of the Institut de France,[20] or was he acting out of loyalty to the image that the order gave of itself under the Ancien Regime: that of a "society of friends" and "thinkers" who respected the throne and the altar? Did Sacy, a Legitimist and a Christian, think that the Masonic ideal might escape the social and political upheaval introduced into the lodges by the Revolution and the Empire? For him, the Restoration, which he welcomed with enthusiasm, undoubtedly promised not only political and religious renewal in France, but also a return to a more traditional view of Freemasonry. Is there any more powerful symbol of this Masonic "restoration" than the replacement, after 1815, in all French lodges, of the bust of Napoleon Bonaparte by that of Louis le Désirée, a ceremony perhaps attended by our Orientalist?

Although we do not know Sacy's exact attitude towards Freemasonry, we can at least gain some idea of what his Masonic practice under the Empire was like (or

to be exact, what it was not like) in that it remains enigmatic—because it was nonexistent. In fact, the only evidence we have of Sacy's Masonic practice is his name, cited three times in the yearbooks from 1809 to 1818. However, he does not appear in the minutes register of the Scottish Mother Lodge from 1808 to 1817, and his signature is never present alongside those of his brothers.[21] So the Orientalist did not frequent his lodge. Yet Sacy had been a Freemason for some time, and we would expect to find him among the dignitaries of the obedience, or decorated with the highest degrees of the philosophical rite that it administered. However, this is not the case. What does this absence tell us? What immediately comes to mind is the complexity and richness of the Orientalist scholar's life: an organized and very full life, with few gaps, a life shared between his home, his study, the Ecole spéciale des langues orientales, the Collège de France, the Institut de France, certain ministries, and his Saint Sulpice parish.[22] It seems unlikely that our indefatigable scholar had enough free time to attend lodge meetings and their lavish banquets.

Moreover, there is no evidence of Sacy's presence at the major events in the history of his obedience. The first of these, in March 1808, was Jean-Jacques-Régis Cambacérès's "installation to the Dignity of Grand Master" of the Mother Lodge. Cambacérès was already Grand Master of

---

[20] See Jean-Michel Léniaud, "Joachim Le Breton et Antoine Quatremère de Quincy, secrétaires perpétuels de l'Académie des Beaux-Arts: deux conceptions divergentes du musée," in *Jean-Baptiste Wicar et son temps, 1762–1834*, ed. Maria Teresa Caracciolo and Gennaro Toscano (Villeneuve d'Arcq: Presses universitaires du Septentrion, 2007), 79–91; Thierry Zarcone, "Les Francs-Maçons de l'Institut d'Egypte et de l'Institut de France, 1798–1815 (l'orientalisme en franc-maçonnerie II)," in preparation.

[21] BnF FM [1] 295.

[22] Reinaud, *Notice historique et littéraire sur M. le Baron Silvestre de Sacy*, 53–54.

the Grand Orient de France, archchancellor of the Empire, and Napoleon's right-hand man.[23] Above all, Sylvestre de Sacy's name is notably absent from the minutes of the "solemn session for the reception into the order of freemasons of Brother Askeri-Khan, ambassador of Persia to the Court of France," which took place in 1808, within the Mother Lodge. Yet this event left a lasting mark on the history of this obedience.[24] One might imagine that Sacy would have attended such an occasion, and perhaps he was pushed to by the dignitaries of the Mother Lodge: undoubtedly, many would have liked to see the Collège de France's famous professor of Persian recognize the representative of the Persian Empire as his Masonic brother. That said, Sacy never hid the fact that he spoke none of the languages he taught—neither Arabic nor Persian.[25] He would therefore have been incapable, in the presence of his brothers, of talking to the prince in his own language. During the ceremony, the ambassador was in fact accompanied by his translator, "Brother [Antoine] Yhary, who had been initiated as a Freemason fourteen days before, for the occasion.[26] Yhary was presented as "inter-

preter-secretary of France, attached to the Persian Legation."[27] Other connoisseurs of Oriental languages were present at the ceremony: Louis-Antoine Vasse, "first dragoman of the General Consulate in Cairo" and the vice-consul of France in Bagdad, and Georges Outrey, a specialist in Iranian affairs and old acquaintance of the ambassador, who was received as a Freemason on the same day. There is no doubt about the political nature of this ceremony organized by an obedience under Cambacérès; it had the unspoken goal of consolidating relationships between the Persian emissary and French politicians and diplomats.[28] The objective was no more and no less than to integrate the Persian prince into the most prestigious "club" that these figures frequented.

There may be another explanation for Sacy's absence at the initiation ceremony for the Persian ambassador. We know that several Ancien Régime Freemasons were uneasy after returning to their Masonic activities from 1800. The spirit had changed, because imperial Freemasonry was beginning a radical transformation of the order, abandoning some of its fun-

---

[23] *Précis historique de la fête donnée à S.A.S. M.gr le Prince Cambacérès, Archi-Chancelier de l'Empire, dans le sein de la R.·. [espectable] Mère Loge Ecossaise de France, sous les titres distinctifs de St-Alexandre d'Ecosse et le Contrat Social réunis, à l'Orient de Paris, le 30 mars 1807* (Paris: l'Imprimerie du F.·. [rère] Caillot, n.d.).

[24] See BnF FM ¹ 295, minutes of November 24, 1808 (4 pp.); Tableau des Frères MLE 1809 (Scottish Mother Lodge Table of Brothers 1809), 11–58; and Annales Maç. MLE 1809 (Scottish Mother Lodge Masonic Annals 1809), 74–93. On this subject, see: François Collavéri, "La Courte Aventure diplomatique et maçonnique d'Askeri Khan, ambassadeur persan—1808–1809," *Points de Vue Initiatiques* 27–28 (1978): 41–69, Tuchendler, "Histoire abrégée de la R. L. Saint Alexandre d'Écosse de l'Ancien Régime à la restauration," 111–88; and Thierry Zarcone, "Comment peut-on être Persan et franc-maçon? L'Ambassadeur Askeri Khan à Paris en 1808-1810," *Revue Jean Erigène* 8 (2009): 183–97.

[25] Cited in Derenbourg, "Esquisse biographique," xviii–xix.

[26] BnF FM ¹ 295, minutes of November 10, 1808.

[27] Annales Maç. MLE 1809 (Scottish Mother Lodge Masonic Annals 1809), 80.

[28] On the political dimension of this event, see Zarcone, "Comment peut-on être Persan et franc-maçon?"

damental principles. Sacy, who, like the Ancien Régime Freemasons, respected the Church and his kingdom, was undoubtedly very wary of this new Freemasonry, which moreover was only a reflection of a political system and a society that he severely criticized. If Sacy did not abandon the Masonic order at this time, and if his name does not disappear from the Mother Lodge lists until 1818, I believe it is because our scholar still had some respect for this ancient and venerable society. However, he undoubtedly did not welcome its political exploitation by the Empire, the reception of the Persian ambassador being an example of this.

## From the Ancient Mysteries to Freemasonry: Clermont-Lodève de Sainte-Croix and Sylvestre de Sacy

It is surprising that Sylvestre de Sacy, who never wrote about the history or rites of Freemasonry, nevertheless indirectly inspired many other Masonic authors. These writers often cite two of his writings, one devoted to the Ancient Mysteries, and the other to the Islamic Druze current. The first is actually a revised edition (with considerable corrections and even some rewritings by Sacy) of a book by his friend Guilhem Clermont-Lodève de Sainte-Croix (1746–1809): *Recherches historiques et critiques sur les mystères du paganisme* (1817) (*Historical Research and Criticism on the Mysteries of Paganism*).[29] A scholar from Provence, who was passionate, among other things, about the history of the ancient religions, Sainte-Croix had an exceptionally rich library, which was auctioned in Paris. Sacy drew up the catalog, and wrote a biography of the author as an introduction to it.[30]

The first version of Sainte-Croix's work, published in 1784 under the title *Mémoires pour servir à l'histoire de la religion secrète des anciens peuples ou Recherches historiques sur les mystères du paganisme* (Paris: Nyon l'aîné) (*Memoirs to Serve the History of the Secret Religion of the Ancient Peoples or Historical Research on the Mysteries of Paganism*), presents a few surprising details not seen in Sacy's revised version. Sainte-Croix compares the ancient initiations, in particular those of Eleusis, Isis, and Mithra, with the initiation in Masonic lodges. He writes:

> We must believe that all the mystagogue's questions and the recipient's answers were set, much like in the catechism of our Freemasons. It changes for the different degrees, and this must also have been the case for the great mysteries of Eleusis and the small mysteries of Agra. [31]

In the last chapter of his work, entitled "On the Total Decadence of the Mysteries," Sainte-Croix observes that "the Kabbalists

---

[29] Second edition revised and corrected by M. le Baron Silvestre de Sacy (Paris: De Bure Frères, 1817, 2 vols).

[30] *Catalogue des livres de la bibliothèque de feu Guilhem Clermont Lodève de Sainte-Croix* (Paris: de Bure, 1809); the "Notice sur M. de Sainte-Croix" ("Notice on M. de Sainte-Croix") is on pages III–XXIV. See also Maurice Larroutis, "Le Baron de Sainte-Croix (1746–1809), un Comtadin injustement oublié," *Mémoires de l'Académie de Vaucluse*, 7th series, tome III (1982): 211–223.

[31] Sainte-Croix, *Mémoires pour servir à l'histoire de la religion secrète*, 185–186.

are as worthy as they [the ancient initiates] are of being considered mysterious sects."[32] He then adds:

> The Druzi, or Druze of Syria, still have one. Its members give Mohammed the name of Satan, and only recognize each other using an enigmatic formula. The first to meet another asks: *In your country is the seed of Halalidge, or the Myrobalan, sown?* If he answers, *It is sown in the hearts of the faithful*, he is immediately recognized as a Brother. Our brave but ignorant knights take from this country the idea of a secret association, and we vainly dispute with them the claim to be its first Authors. Different aspects of it could well have clear relationships with the fables of Osiris and Horus, or with the tragic death of the young Iacchus. The questions asked of modern Recipients, and their answers, are very similar to those of the mysteries of Eleusis, and are no more than the use of foreign and Oriental words, as observed by M. de Villoison. Do they not imitate the language of the Sybil, perhaps used in the ancient initiations?[33]

In a long footnote, Sainte-Croix cites Anse de Villoison, who established a parallel between "these terrifying trials imposed on the recipient," or future Freemason, and those undergone by the initiate in the Ancient Mysteries. He also establishes a parallel between the Freemason's skin apron and the "fawn skin" that "was habitually mystical." Belle-Croix indicates that the source used by Villoison is a work of Masonic revelation entitled *Les Plus Secrets Mystères des hauts-grades de la maçonnerie dévoilés, ou le vrai rose-croix, traduit de l'anglais, suivi du Noachite, avec figures* (Jerusalem, 1768) (*The Most Secret Mysteries of the High Degrees of Masonry Revealed, or the True Rosy-Cross, Translated from the English, Followed by the Noachite, with Figures*). This booklet, the first edition of which was published in 1766, was a best-seller in eighteenth-century bookshops.[34] Belle-Croix concludes his work with a rather sibylline phrase, using the citation from Friedrich Wilhelm Gotter's booklet l*es N.N. ou sur les inconnus* (1777), which connects the Templars to the Ancient Mysteries and the Freemasons:

> A Scholar received in our Lodges cries "Let us complete this edifice to virtue that we build in our hearts! It is the first of our principles, from which all the others are derived" [*Essai sur les N.N. ou sur les inconnus*]. If the brothers want to work seriously on this great task, it will undoubtedly only be by strengthening social ties, constantly weakened by selfishness.

Yet these passages and the accompanying notes are absent from the newer edition of the work, having been removed by Sacy. He undoubtedly considered that the references to the Templars and to Freemasonry were not pertinent, and that the

---

[32] Sainte-Croix, *Mémoires pour servir à l'histoire de la religion secrète*, 509.

[33] Sainte-Croix, *Mémoires pour servir à l'histoire de la religion secrète*, 509-511.

[34] Sainte-Croix, *Mémoires pour servir à l'histoire de la religion secrète*, 510.

*Plus Secrets Mystères des hauts-grades de la maçonnerie dévoilés*, a simple work of revelation, as well as the *Essai sur les N.N. ou sur les inconnus*, had no scientific value. Moreover, Sacy was uneasy with the reference to the Templars, as I will show later in this paper. In the 1817 edition of Sainte-Croix's book, Sacy nevertheless kept the reference to contemporary "famous and mysterious associations"—clearly a reference to Freemasonry. He edited and corrected the text, removing the last part of the final phrase, which confirms that Freemasonry could be one of the "famous and mysterious associations" in question by mentioning the existence of several degrees.

Yet these passages and the accompanying notes are absent from the newer edition of the work, having been removed by Sacy. He undoubtedly considered that the references to the Templars and to Freemasonry were not pertinent, and that the Plus Secrets Mystères des hauts-grades de la maçonnerie dévoilés, a simple work of revelation, as well as the Essai sur les N.N. ou sur les inconnus, had no scientific value. Moreover, Sacy was uneasy with the reference to the Templars, as I will show later in this paper. In the 1817 edition of Sainte-Croix's book, Sacy nevertheless kept the reference to contemporary "famous and mysterious associations"—clearly a reference to Freemasonry. He edited and corrected the text, removing the last part of the final phrase, which confirms that Freemasonry could be one of the "famous and mysterious associations" in question by mentioning the existence of several degrees.

| 1784 edition (page 511): | 1817 edition (vol. 1, pages 346–347): |
|---|---|
| "It is plausible that after this proclamation, those present were asked again to make an inviolable vow of secrecy, which they were obliged to keep. They were then asked, either individually or as a group: Have you eaten bread? Each would answer: *No, I have drunk kykeon; I have taken cistus; after working, I put it into the calathus, then calathus into the cistus*; which proved that they had been admitted to the small mysteries. If, in answer to the first question, someone simply said, "Yes," they would be unmasked. This way of telling profanes from Adepts, and combating indiscreet curiosity, is so natural that we still see it used in famous and mysterious associations, when their members are promoted to different degrees." | "It is plausible that after this proclamation, those attending were asked again to make a vow of inviolable secrecy. They were then asked, as for the small mysteries, either individually or as a group: *Have you eaten bread? etc. Each would answer: I have fasted and I have drunk kykeon; I have taken cistus and put it into the calathus, I have received it again and carried it in the little cistus.* All this related to Ceres, and to what the mystery had done before. If, in answer to the first question, someone simply answered, "Yes," they would unmask themselves. This way of telling profanes from Adepts, and combating indiscreet curiosity, is so natural that we still see it used in famous and mysterious associations." |

Sainte-Croix's work, as revised, amended, critiqued, restructured, and rid of all direct reference to Freemasonry by Sacy, nevertheless undeniably marked Freemasons in its century, who were seeking the meaning behind their mysteries and rites and keen to link them directly to antiquity. "Initiations hold a distinguished place in the august order of Masonry. They characterize its ancient and sublime nature," wrote Brother Caignard de Mailly, a member of the Mother Lodge, in 1809.[35] Another Freemason and a contemporary of Sacy, who was a member of the same obedience, cites Sainte-Croix several times, in a study undoubtedly presented at the lodge and entitled "Des Mystères d'Eleusis" ("On the Mysteries of Eleusis").[36] In addition to this, the fourth section of the Mother Lodge's library is devoted "to the works of ancient and modern philosophers, from whom the Freemasons drew their mysteries, or in whom they thought they recognized them." It is specified that these works include the "works of Sainte-Croix" and "the Ezour-Vedam, or ancient Commentary on the Vedam, by M. de Sainte-Croix."[37] The *Recherches historiques et critiques sur les mystères du paganisme* remained authoritative in Masonic circles throughout the nineteenth century. For example, the work is mentioned, in 1853, in a publication by the very productive Masonic author Jean-Marie Ragon, *Orthodoxie maçonnique suivi de la maçonnerie occulte et de l'initiation hermétique* (*Masonic Orthodoxy Followed by the Occult Masonry and the Hermetic Initiation*).[38]

## Druze and Masonic Initiations

We have seen above that the final pages of *Mémoires pour servir à l'histoire de la religion secrète des anciens peuples* refer to the Syrian Druze movement, which the author also considers to be one of the "mysterious sects." Again, sections have been removed from Sainte-Croix's text. Sacy eliminates another reference to Anse de Villoison, as well as a comment from the author. Nevertheless, like Sainte-Croix, he retains the idea (explained further on) that there are striking similarities between the Ancient Mysteries and a modern association that clearly refers to Freemasonry.

Sainte-Croix's mention of the Druze prompts a long footnote from Sacy. The note offers additional information on the Islamic movement, as well as on Muslim mystics or "sufis," because, Sacy writes, they, like the Druze, had a "secret doctrine."[39] On the Druze, the Orientalist notes that they are a "degenerate branch" of the

---

[35] Caignard de Mailly, "Coup d'oeil sur les anciennes initiations," in Annales Maç. MLE 1807 (Scottish Mother Lodge Masonic Annals 1807), 11.

[36] A. B., "Des Mystères d'Eleusis," in Annales Maç. MLE 1807 (Scottish Mother Lodge Masonic Annals 1807), 31, 41, 54, 81.

[37] Annuaire Maç. MLE 1811 (Scottish Mother Lodge Masonic Yearbook 1811), 96–97.

[38] Jean-Marie Ragon, *Orthodoxie maçonnique suivi de la maçonnerie occulte et de l'initiation hermétique*, (Paris: E. Dentu, 1853), 287.

[39] Guilhem Clermont-Lodève de Sainte-Croix, *Recherches historiques et critiques sur les mystères du paganisme*, 2:196–97.

| 1784 edition (page 511): | 1817 edition (vol. 2, page 198) |
|---|---|
| "The questions asked of modern Recipients, and their answers, are very similar to those of the mysteries of Eleusis, and are no more than the use of foreign and Oriental words, as observed by M. de Villoison. Do they not imitate the language of the Sybil, perhaps used in the ancient initiations?" | "The questions asked of the Recipients, and their answers, recall practices regarding the mysteries of Eleusis. The use of barbarian formulae and words, or words borrowed from the languages of the Orient offers a further and rather striking similarity with the Ancient Mysteries, and can indicate the foreign and Oriental origin of these modern associations." |

Ismaili, and that they have "a system of initiation in seven degrees, to which a person was only admitted after many tests." Sacy knew this subject perfectly, having studied it for over fifteen years. Much later, in articles on the monumental work devoted to this question, he would write that this religious movement belonged to "the history of aberrations of the human mind."[40] Our Orientalist therefore had no sympathy for the Druze, unlike many of the Freemasons throughout the nineteenth and twentieth centuries, who saw the secret religion as the oriental twin of the Masonic order, and his partisans as the descendants of the builders of the Temple of Solomon. Several travelers and scholars share this opinion, such as the German Joseph von Hammer-Purgstall, who thought he had shown, in his 1818 *Die Geschichte der Assassinen*, the existence of a historical filiation between the Ismaili, the Druze, the Templars, and the Freemasons.[41] The myth of the Druze origins of Freemasonry is in part built on Hammer-Purgstall's works, as well as on those of Sacy, despite him being far from supportive of the German scholar's

---

[40] Silvestre de Sacy, "Recherches sur l'initiation à la secte des Ismaéliens," *Journal asiatique* 4 (1824): 298. See also Silvestre de Sacy, *Exposé de la religion des Druzes, tiré des livres religieux de cette secte et précédé d'une introduction et de la vie du Khalife Hakem-Biamr-Allah* (Paris: Imprimerie royale, 1838): 2 vols.

[41] The book was translated into French in 1833: J. J. Hellert and Propser Alexis Gaubert de la Nourais, trans., *Histoire de l'ordre des assassins* (Paris: Paulin, 1833).

[42] See Daniel De Smet, "Les Prétendues Origines druzes de la franc-maçonnerie. Naissance et persistance d'un mythe," in *Traces de l'Autre. Mythes de l'antiquité et peuples du Livre dans la construction des nations méditerranéennes*, ed. Josiane Boulad-Ayouba and Gian Mario Cazzaniga (Paris-Pisa: Vrin, 2004), 261–74.

theories.[42]

Hammer, enemy of secret societies and Freemasonry (he admits that one of the objectives of his work is to "show the disastrous influence of secret societies under weak governments")[43] made the French and German theories (which we know to be unfounded) his own, attributing a revolutionary culture of subversion to the Freemasons and the Illuminati, with secrecy serving to conceal their anti-monarchic and antireligious work.[44] The German Orientalist openly confirms his opinion and clearly targets the Freemasons in his 1818 book on the Baphomet of the Templars, *Mysterium Baphometi revelatum* (*The Mysteries of Baphomet Revealed*).[45] Hammer therefore finds it natural for European secret societies and the Druze to share an attraction to plotting and a hatred of kings and religions. Sacy thinks the opposite, and clearly expresses his disagreement with the German scholar in his critical summary of Hammer's work in 1818:

It is impossible to study with any degree of attention the history of the Assassins, and in general the histories of the Ismaili, without noticing the many strongly characterized links existing between this sect or secret association and the Order of the Templars, as

well as more modern secret societies, which seem to have followed on from this order; links which lie in the organization and hierarchy, the doctrine, the practices, the external forms, the forms of expression, etc. Nevertheless, I do not know if Mr. de Hammer will be thought sufficiently justified, by these incontestable links, in transporting to the sect of the Assassins the denominations of Order, Lodge, Grand Master, Grand Prior, etc., borrowed from the military orders of the West.[46]

Sacy does acknowledge the real resemblances between the Druze, the Templars, and "more modern secret societies," but he does not acknowledge any historical filiation between these groups, or Hammer's free attribution of terms used in the European military orders and in Freemasonry to the Druze. Above all, he rejects Hammer's explanations for these similarities:

Nor do I believe that a right-minded critique would adopt all the rapprochements hazarded by Mr. de Hammer, between the Ismaili, the Templars, the Freemasons, the Jesuits, the Illuminati, and the modern associations that either provoked or favored the over-

---

[43] Joseph Von Hammer-Purgstall, *Histoire de l'ordre des assassins*, 341.

[44] See the clarification in Pierre-Yves Beaurepaire, L'*Europe des francs-maçons, XVIIIe–XXIe siècles* (Paris: Belin, 2002), 146–68.

[45] Edited in Wenceslas Riewufky, ed. *Fundgruben des Orient bearbeitet durch eine Gesellschaft von Liebhabern - Mines de l'Orient, exploitées par une société d'amateurs*, vol. 6 (Vienna: Gedruckt Bey Anton Schmid, K. K. Privil und N. Ö. Landschafts Buchdrucker, 1818).

[46] Sylvestre de Sacy, "Die Geschichte der Assassinen, aus morgenlandischen Quellen, durch Joseph von Hammer. - L'Histoire des Assassins," *Journal des Savants* 8 (1818): 413–4.

throw of the altar and the throne. Some of these rapprochements would appear forced to an impartial reader, and it would be enough to give a glimpse of the others.[47]

Sacy therefore clearly disagrees with Hammer's theory that Freemasonry shares a hatred of royalty and the Church with the Druze. On this point, the German scholar is very clear, and without citing the Freemasons, makes indirect reference to them, writing: "[The first perpetrators of] the French Revolution . . . were the members of secret societies, who, like the Ismaili, wanted only to overthrow thrones and altars."[48] Sacy, who frequented the French lodges under the Ancien Régime, was undoubtedly convinced that they had never been the antechambers of revolutionary action, because if they had, as a monarchist and Christian, he would never have agreed to appear as a Freemason in the yearbook of a Masonic obedience after the Revolution. Other Freemasons, such as Huvier des Fontenelle or Gauthier de Brécy, who like our Orientalist were initiated under the Ancien Régime, and who returned to the lodges from 1800, stated that the Revolution was not the work of the brothers.[49] In 1834, Gauthier de Brécy wrote:

I will give no time here to either the reality or the merits of the supposed secrets of the Masonic order; but I am convinced of the purity of the sentiments professed there, and I challenge anyone to prove that they ever carried out any act against the interests of religion, the throne, and morality.[50]

Sylvestre de Sacy became involved in Freemasonry at the end of the eighteenth century, like many notables, nobles, and Parisian or provincial bourgeois citizens, seeking a "pleasant, social pastime" or an elite club, or even a society of thought or a sanctuary devoted to friendship. It was perhaps colleagues at the Cour des Monnaies or family relations who brought him there. However, the Orientalist did not abandon the order after 1789, unlike many other Freemasons. He maintained his links with Freemasonry and, under the Empire and the Restoration, even allowed his name to be listed in the yearbooks of an obedience: a sign of his continuing loyalty. But Sacy did not participate in the life of the lodges or the obedience, despite the fact that his writings indirectly defend the image of a Freemasonry innocent of plotting, which respected its king and its Church. In spite of his loyalty to the order, did he ultimately prefer the fraternity con-

---

[47] De Sacy, "Die Geschichte der Assassinen, aus morgenlandischen Quellen, durch Joseph von Hammer," 415.

[48] Hammer-Purgstall, *Histoire de l'ordre des assassins*, 82.

[49] See Jean-Marie Mercier, "L'Univers culturel et intellectuel d'un franc-maçon de province sous l'Empire. Textes et chansons du frère Huvier des Fontenelles," in *La Franc-Maçonnerie sous l'Empire: un âge d'or?* (Paris: Dervy, 2007), 241–92; Thierry Zarcone, "Gauthier de Brécy, Charles Edme, Vicomte de (1753–1836)," in *Le Monde maçonnique des Lumières (Europe-Amériques). Dictionnaire prosopographique*, ed. Charles Porcet and Cécile Révauger (Paris: Honoré Champion, forthcoming).

[50] Gauthier de Brécy, *Mémoires véridiques et ingénues de la vie privée, morale et politique d'un homme de bien* (Paris: Imprimerie de Giraudet, 1834), 118.

necting him to his "brothers" at the Institut de France to that of his Masonic brothers? Three of his students at the Ecole spéciale des langues orientales and the Collège de France also joined Freemasonry under the Consulate and became members of the Scottish Mother Lodge of France. Moreover, they were important figures: Henri-Nicolas Belleteste and Louis-Rémy Raige, who contributed to the *Description de l'Egypte* (*Description of Egypt*), and Pierre-Amédée Jaubert, who succeeded Sacy at the Collège de France.[51] Did they meet with their professor at the lodge, or discuss the "mysteries" of their society with him? Did they share their experiences as both Orientalists and Masonic brothers? Did they share the same Masonic ideal? The ambiguity of Sylvestre de Sacy's Masonic career leaves many questions unanswered, and we can hope that in the future, new or still little-known documents might shed light on this "secret life," which my brief study has sadly only partly uncovered.

---

[51] On these three figures in Orientalism, see Thierry Zarcone, "Les Francs-Maçons de l'Institut d'Egypte et de l'Institut de France, 1798–1815 (l'orientalisme en franc-maçonnerie II)," (forthcoming).